GROWING IN THE SPIRIT

Other titles by D Martyn Lloyd-Jones

Joy Unspeakable
Prove All Things
The Cross
Healing and Medicine
Saved in Eternity (Spiritual Assurance: 1)
Safe in the World (Spiritual Assurance: 2)
Sanctified Through the Truth (Spiritual Assurance: 3)

SPIRITUAL ASSURANCE: 4

Growing in the Spirit

D MARTYN LLOYD-JONES

Edited by Christopher Catherwood

KINGSWAY PUBLICATIONS
EASTBOURNE

Front cover photo by Tony Stone Photolibrary – London

British Library Cataloguing in Publication Data

Lloyd-Jones, D.M. (David Martyn), *1899–1981*
    Growing in the spirit
    1. Christian doctrine. Holy Spirit
    I. Title
    231′.3

ISBN 0–86065–763–9

Printed in Great Britain for
KINGSWAY PUBLICATIONS LTD
1 St Anne's Road, Eastbourne, E.Sussex BN21 3UN by
Richard Clay Ltd, Bungay, Suffolk.
Typeset by Watermark, Hampermill Cottage, Watford WD1 4PL

Contents

1

'Take Time to be Holy'

Sanctify them through thy truth: thy word is truth (John 17:17).

These words are an extraordinary and most comprehensive pet-ition offered by our Lord and Saviour Jesus Christ on behalf of his immediate followers and disciples, and, indeed, on behalf of all his followers and disciples in all ages and in all places. We have been expounding verse 17 in detail, because it is one of the crucial petitions in this high-priestly prayer which our Lord offered and which is recorded in John chapter 17.[1] He is con-cerned about these people not only because of themselves, but because he is leaving them in the world to do certain work. He reminds his Father that as his Father has sent him into the world, so he is sending them into the world; it is for this reason that he prays that they may be kept from the Evil One, and, further, and positively, that they may be sanctified. We have looked in particular at the method of sanctification as it is here taught by our Lord, and as it is taught everywhere in the Scriptures. 'Sanctify them,' he says, 'through thy truth.' Bring them into the realm of the truth; keep them there so that the Truth shall work upon them and influence them and produce their sanctifi-cation.

Furthermore, we have been at pains to emphasise that this process of sanctification depends finally and essentially upon

---

[1] See Vol. 3, *Sanctified Through the Truth* (Kingsway Publications 1988).

7

our understanding of what this truth is. Our Lord says, 'Thy word is truth,' so the way to be sanctified is to look at this word and to receive it. And we have seen that it is a great word and a great truth which can be divided into certain central propositions. The whole word itself is something which promotes our sanctification, but there are certain aspects, certain emphases, which are of particular importance and significance, and we have looked at six of them. These, I would suggest to you, are the six main aspects of this great truth of our salvation. First is the truth about God himself: we must ever start there, everything in connection with our salvation concerns our relationship to God. To be saved is not primarily to be happy, it is not primarily to have an experience; the essence of salvation is that we are in the right relationship to God. From the beginning, the great promise of God with regard to salvation is this: 'I will be your God, and ye shall be my people' (eg Lev 26:7), so if we find that our tendency is to view salvation in any way except directly in terms of our knowledge of God and our relationship to him, it is a false tendency. We must ever be careful to avoid that subtle temptation and we must never be tired of reminding ourselves of the danger of being too subjective.

We might, I know, immediately add that there is an equal danger of being too objective, but let us remember that both are true, and perhaps the greater danger is that of being too subjective. We are living in a difficult world. The times are cruel; we are all tired as the result of wars and the uncertainty that has followed this last world war, and the craving at the present time is for some release and quiet. We require that subjectively and that is quite a good thing, but we must be very careful lest we put it in the first position and fail to realise that the thing which, after all, marks and differentiates the Christian is that he is someone who is in a given relationship to God. The great doctrine of God, the being and character of God, must override everything else. The whole purpose of the Bible is to reveal God to us and to bring us into communion with him, which is the life eternal. Why? So that I should be happy? No! '...that they might know thee the only true God, and Jesus Christ, whom thou hast sent'

(Jn 17:3). That leads to untold happiness and the greatest bliss imaginable, but there are times when it leads to trembling and to fear and drives us to Christ.

Having looked at that, we then went on to look at the doctrine of sin, so that we might see man as he really is in the sight of God; and all this promotes our sanctification. From that, we looked at what God has done for us in our sin, the doctrine of the sending of his Son into the world, and especially his death upon the cross, that amazing action whereby we are purchased and reconciled, redeemed and rescued – all that is absolutely vital to the doctrine of sanctification. And our emphasis there was that we must never regard the cross as something that belongs to the initial stages of our Christian life; we must never get the impression that we have passed by the cross. No, we do not go on from the cross to sanctification, but we find our sanctification in the cross. It is by the precious blood of Christ that we have been purchased, we are not our own – that is sanctification.

Then, having laid down the great fundamental proposition of our fall, we went on to see how Scripture, particularly in this matter of sanctification, introduces us to the great doctrine of our identification with Christ and of the fact that we are in Christ. And from there we considered the truth that always should be taken with that: that Christ is also in us. We are in him and he in us – how astounding that is! Then we considered the relevance of the doctrine concerning the Resurrection to this question of our sanctification. The argument, according to 1 Corinthians 15, is not that the doctrine of the Resurrection is only a comfort to those who are dying or bereaved, it is not something that we should rejoice in on one Sunday in the year only – rushing to church on that Sunday, then neglecting to go again until the next Easter Sunday comes along. No, says the Apostle, in the light of this doctrine, 'Therefore,' and the 'therefore' leads to concentration upon daily life and living: '...be ye stedfast, unmoveable, always abounding in the work of the Lord' (1 Cor 15:58); 'evil communications corrupt good manners' (1 Cor 15:33). So we must 'awake to righteousness and sin not' (v. 34); and we must go on to labour and to realise that our labour is not in vain in the Lord. Those, then, are the great fundamental doctrines, and our sanctification is ever, always, the result of our realisation of them.

So having laid this down, we now come to a more practical aspect of this whole matter. 'Sanctify them,' says our Lord, 'through [or in] thy truth.' But before that can happen, we have to learn that this great, vital truth, at which we have been looking, is something that must of necessity be constantly applied by us, and that the application of the truth is quite as important as the truth itself. There is no value whatsoever in having an intellectual awareness of the truth unless we proceed to apply it, and there are many who fail at that point. So I want now to come to this truth and to its application, and if you read Romans 6 you will see that this is precisely what the apostle Paul does. In the previous chapters he has been laying down his great doctrine of justification by faith only. He has been demonstrating it from the Scriptures, making it perfectly plain and clear. So he has stated the doctrine, but, wise teacher as he is, he knows that men and women in a state of sin and under the influence and at the suggestion of the devil, are liable to fail to apply it at all, or to apply it in the wrong way.

Now the Christians in Rome, having heard the doctrines of justification by faith only, of their union with Christ, and incorporation into him – as you were once in Adam, Paul has just taught them in chapter 5, so you are now in Christ; and as the result of Adam's transgression came upon you, so everything that Christ has done has happened to you – having heard this, they might come to a wrong conclusion. Paul realises that some might say, 'Very well, then, if that is so, it does not matter what we do.' They might even say, 'The more we sin the greater will grace abound, or the more we sin the more grace will show itself, therefore let us continue in sin.' And, immediately, he rejects this with abhorrence and alarm, and proceeds to work out this great argument in Romans 6, the essence of which is that, in a final sense, you must not divide justification and sanctification. For the man who realises truly what it is to be justified, is one who realises the absolute necessity of sanctification.

Let me put that in a slightly different form. I want to suggest to you that it is not enough, even, to be aware of this great doctrine; but before our sanctification can proceed, these doctrines must be applied. There are many ways in which we can apply them. One way is to consider together what it means to walk and live by faith. William Romaine, a great evangelical clergyman who lived in London some two hundred years ago, published a book which he called *The Life and Walk and Triumph of Faith*. This title correctly indicates that the whole of the Christian life is a life of faith. We walk by faith not by sight – all the great doctrines are held by faith and as Christians we must view our life in this world as a walk, as a great progression in this life of faith.

But people encounter many difficulties with regard to this life, and I want to mention two of them in particular. Furthermore, I shall deal with them purely on a practical level because any preacher who is not practical is not a true preacher of the gospel. The first danger is that of imagining that because we have believed, because we are Christians, these truths are going to apply themselves automatically in our lives. That is a great fallacy. Faith is not passive, it is very active. We must, it is true, always be aware of the danger of relying upon our own activity, but the opposite of that is not just to do nothing! Faith is active. The first step in the life of faith is the constant application of the truth which we have believed, the bringing to bear upon our daily lives of these great doctrines which we have been studying. That is the first thing. In other words, we must not wait for some great experience. Rather, if we want the great experience, the thing to do is to apply what we believe. Then we shall receive it.

The second difficulty which people encounter with regard to the sanctified Christian life is this: they expect to feel something special happening to them. We must learn that sanctification is not so much a matter of feeling and sensibility, as the application of the truth which we have believed. This is almost a constant problem. We all seem instinctively to desire to have the feeling before we believe, and there are large numbers of people who spend years in waiting and pleading for some particular sensation, some experience. The argument is: 'If only I knew these things, if only I were absolutely certain, if only I could experience what I read has happened to others, then I would live the "sanctified life".' So they wait for an experience which never seems to come, and the result is that their lives are bound in shallows and miseries. And there again is this same fallacy, for the Christian life is a walk of faith, it is a life of faith. The feelings may come and they may go, but the walk of faith must always continue. The Bible does not say anywhere that whosoever *feeleth* certain things shall be saved, but whosoever *believeth*, and we must grasp that. We must not be waiting for these sensations and feelings, but, having looked at these great doctrines, we must proceed to walk in them, to live by them, and to apply them to our daily life.

What does this actually mean in practice? Let me try to summarise like this. First and foremost, of course, we must familiarise ourselves with the doctrine. That almost goes without saying. If we are not aware of these doctrines we cannot live by them. We must believe them and we must accept them. There is no Christian life at all apart from that. We must accept these doctrines because they are revealed in the word of God, the same word of truth of which our Lord speaks. So we start there; but that is not enough. The point I want to emphasise in particular here is that we must constantly remind ourselves of them. I can best put it in the words of Romans 6:11: 'Likewise reckon ye also yourselves to be dead indeed unto sin, but alive unto God through Jesus Christ our Lord.' That is what we must do, and the life of faith, the walk of faith, the life of sanctification, is, in reality, just that – reckoning ourselves to be dead indeed unto sin but alive unto God in and through Jesus Christ our Lord.

How, then, do I remind myself in this way? Let us be perfectly simple and practical. The most essential step is constantly to read the Scriptures. If you look at any saint who has ever adorned the life of the Christian church, you will find that they

have always done that. They have always been men and women
who have spent a great deal of their time in reading the Bible,
studying it and familiarising themselves with it.

Once again I want to issue a very important warning. There
are many ways of reading the Bible, and I mean reading it in a
very particular way. I have known people who seem to read
their Bible like this: they say, 'Yes, I am now a Christian. I
believe in the Lord Jesus Christ and have surrendered myself to
him. I have had this experience.' So now they seem to be living
on that experience and they believe that henceforth they have
nothing to do but look to him.

'Well then,' you say, 'do you not read your Bible?'

'O yes,' they reply, 'I read my Bible.'

But they seem to read the Bible as a good bit of discipline, as
the sort of thing a Christian is expected to do. That is not the
way of reading the Bible that I mean here. I am advocating that
I should read my Bible daily not because I believe it is a good
thing for me to read the word every day, not because I think it
is going to do some general good, not because it is a good thing
to be familiar with the word of God – no – I must learn to read
the word of God in order to look for the doctrines that are in it.
I must search for doctrines which I can apply to myself, I must
be looking for particular teachings. My reading of the Bible
must not be general, but very specific.

It is possible to be very familiar with the letter of the Scriptures and yet not to know its doctrines; indeed, there are many
who are familiar with the words of the Scriptures who are not
familiar with the word of God. You can know your Bible in a
mechanical sense without ever having come face to face with its
doctrines. And my whole understanding of John 17:17 leads me
to say that all that is useless. In other words, if I do not read my
Bible in such a way as to come to a deeper knowledge of the
greatness and holiness of God, there is something wrong in my
reading, and the same is true if my reading of the Bible does not
humble me, or bend me to my knees. In other words, my
attitude towards Scripture reading must not be, 'I have a certain
amount of time before I go to work,' or, 'I read my daily portion

if I can' – that is not the way to read the Scriptures. We must be very careful not to become slaves to the daily portion. We must be searching for the doctrines not merely that we may know the contents of particular books of the Bible, but also that its spiritual message may come out to us. We must see it and know it, and we must daily remind ourselves of it.

Every day I must remind myself of God and his character, and of my position as a human being, an inheritor of original sin in Adam, the remnants of which – the pollution of sin – still remain. Day by day, then, I must remind myself of the law and of God's condemnation of sin; I must ever look at the cross, and meditate upon it every day, bringing it constantly before me. You see what I am saying? We all know from experience how easy it is to take these things for granted, and so much for granted that we never stop to think about them at all. Christians are people who live daily in the light of these things; and they must go to the Scriptures more and more frequently in order that they may remind themselves of these things which are so absolutely vital to their sanctification.

Then you must not only read the Scriptures, you must also meditate upon them. There is a line of a hymn which says, 'Take time to be holy.' I am not sure but that it is not something which we all ought to have pasted upon the walls of our homes in this foolish, ridiculous, hectic age in which we are living. We are all involved in this mad rush which is so meaningless. We allow the world to govern us and our time. We say we have no time to do these things I have been talking about – people are not reading the Bible as they used to, because they are doing something else. The hours of work are shorter than they have ever been, so why do we have less time? It is because we are reading other things, for if we spend our time reading journals and magazines, obviously we have no time to read our Bibles, nor do we have time to meditate. Indeed, the art of meditation has practically disappeared out of life; people do not think. As the poet tramp said:

What is this life if, full of care,
We have no time to stand and stare?
>   *W H Davies*

We do not look at things, we do not consider them as we ought, and above all, we fail to meditate upon these spiritual things.

So we must turn them over in our minds – and we have to make ourselves do this; we need discipline. We must confront these things. How easy it is to find that our day has gone before we think it has started – time slips between our fingers and it is gone. The days hurry along and the weeks and the months. We are all hurrying towards the end of our life in this world, and we have not done all that much. We must take hold of ourselves firmly and be drastic with ourselves. We must insist upon these things and make ourselves confront them day by day.

I suggest that this means that we must cultivate the lost art of talking to ourselves. Do not misunderstand me. I do not mean talking to ourselves audibly. But more and more I find that the very essence of the truly spiritual life is that people talk to themselves about these things. It is my business as a preacher not only to preach to others, but to myself also, and the real value of my preaching to others is the extent to which I preach to myself before I preach to them. As I understand this term 'reckon yourself to be dead unto sin', it means that I talk to myself, and I say, 'Do you know who and what you are?' I preach to myself as I get up in the morning and I say, 'You are a creature in this world of time who has been placed in it by Almighty God. You are not merely an animal evolved out of some primitive slime, you are a man made in the image and likeness of God, there is that dignity about you – remember it!'

How easy it is to take a false value of ourselves from the newspapers, or from the way of the world. If we unconsciously tend to do that, our life will not be truly sanctified. So talk to yourself about yourself, and talk to God about yourself. Talk to yourself about sin; examine yourself; view the day that is ahead of you and at night review the day that has gone. Have you ever tried to do that seriously? Have you gone over the day and the things you have done during the day, even the good things you have done? When you examine them, my friends, you may find that you have done even the good things in a very bad way. You have to know yourself, you have to know what you are doing and you talk to yourself about yourself, and then you talk to yourself about the cross, because if you do not talk to yourself about the cross you may go for months and years without knowing anything about it. Remind yourself of what happened there, that the Son of God died and rose again, and say, 'If he rose, I rose with him.' Say that to yourself daily! Remind yourself daily of who and what you are. Talk to yourself, too, about the fleeting character of your life here and about the glory that is coming.

Oh, I do commend this to you. God knows I do so as a man who is a failure himself at doing what he is advocating, but I do it, and I want to do it more and more, and I can assure you that there is nothing so blessed and so rewarding. Have you ever conceived of yourself and thought about yourself in the glory? Have you ever thought of what it is going to be to look into his blessed face and to see him as he is? Remind yourself of these things, reckon yourself to be dead unto sin but alive unto God. Say to yourself that you are only a stranger in this world, a sojourner, a traveller. Tell yourself, 'Heaven is my home, I am a citizen of heaven, I belong there. I daily, nightly, pitch my moving tent a day's march nearer home.' That is what it means to 'reckon yourself dead unto sin'. It is not only that I know the doctrines of justification and sanctification, and something of the doctrine of God. Yes, but what matters is whether I am applying them. Am I living in the light of these things? That is the life and walk of faith. Faith means that this is the truth about me and therefore I live like this.

That, then, is the great emphasis, and from that I must go on to draw certain deductions. First, I must work out this great argument in the same way as the Apostle does in Romans 6. If all this is true, then I am in a very definite and given relationship to God – I am in Christ. This means that I am dead to sin and I am alive unto God. I sometimes think that if we only realised that, we would not need to worry about anything else. It means that God is my Father and I can go immediately into his presence and speak to him in Christ. If only we realised that, there would be no need for us to exhort one another to prayer and to a life of prayer, it would follow inevitably. If only we knew God's love to us; if only we realised that God is indeed our Father; if only we realised that he is interested in us, in everything we are and in all we do to the very smallest, minutest details of our life – even to the numbering of the very hairs of our head – if only we realised all these things, what a difference it would make!

But our problem is that we get up in the morning and there are things to be done. Then we read a hurried word of Scripture and off we go. We might as well not have done it, I am afraid. Rather, we must 'take time to be holy', we must take time to realise what we are doing. If only, when we are on our knees, we could realise what the real truth is at that moment, that the eternal, everlasting God is listening to us, is stooping towards us, waiting to hear what we have to say, waiting, not for our hurried petitions, nor to hear us, like fretful children, asking for this, that and the other; but rather waiting to hear us thanking him, praising his name, loving and adoring him, giving our-selves to him and telling him we want to live day by day to his honour and glory. If only we took time to think like that! For that is real prayer; that is the life of the saint; that is the life of faith and we must take time to remind ourselves of these things – to 'reckon' as Paul tells us.

You may wake up in the morning feeling dry and hard in spirit and absolutely lifeless in a spiritual sense. The reason may be partly physical or any number of other things, and you may feel utterly opposed to real prayer. But it does not matter what you feel. You must say to yourself, 'I reckon myself to be dead to sin and alive to God; I know that this is true and therefore I am going to talk to my Father.' In the natural sense we do not wait to feel like doing things before we do them – at least, I hope we do not. I trust that as husbands and wives and parents and children we do the things that we must do, however we feel.

The same applies to our relationship with God. Reckon yourselves, act on this great truth which you say you believe, and go
into his presence, asking him first and foremost to forgive you
for your dryness and for your lack of a lively sense of the Spirit.
Confess it, acknowledge it, and ask him to give you liberty and
to manifest himself to you. That is the life of faith, and you have
to do it. Do not wait until you are moved; move yourself and
then you will find that the Spirit will be present.

And, secondly, in the same way we are to realise that our life
should consist of walking in the light with him, and that, of
necessity, will lead us to a dedication of ourselves and of our
faculties to him: 'Neither yield ye your members as instruments
of unrighteousness unto sin: but yield yourselves unto God as
those that are alive from the dead, and your members as instruments of righteousness unto God' (Rom 6:13). You go to him
and say: 'Here I am, my body, my mind, my spirit, every
power and faculty which I have. You have given them to me.
I have not generated them, they are gifts from you. I am giving
myself to you from this day, use these gifts, take possession of
them, every faculty I have, let them be used, that you may be
glorified.' You are reckoned to be dead to that selfish life and
you are living to God and righteousness.

And, finally, you draw the deduction that sin is something
which is quite unthinkable. Listen to this: 'What fruit had ye
then in those things whereof ye are now ashamed? for the end
of those things is death' (Rom 6:21). When we are Christians we
have an entirely new view of sin. But it is only as we remind
ourselves of these truths, and apply them to ourselves, and talk
to ourselves about them that these deductions become evident,
and at the same time inevitable.

So let me sum it all up again in that little phrase: 'Take time
to be holy.' It does take time. Read the lives of the greatest saints
this world has ever seen and you will find that they spent hours
every day in reading their Bibles. John Wesley said that he had
a very poor opinion of Christians who did not spend at least four
hours every day in prayer. The great saints agonised and strove
in prayer. Some of them prayed so much that when they got up

from their knees there was a pool of sweat on the ground. Others wore out their chairs or tables, or the oilcloth on the floor (you can see where Henry Martyn did that in Cambridge); that is the life of faith. These people took time to be holy. They did not say, 'It is quite simple, all you have to do is accept it.' They trusted finally, as we must inevitably do, to the action and the power of God. But trusting to that, they studied the word of God and loved it, they laboured, they agonised in prayer, they meditated, and thus they grew in grace and in the knowledge of God, and were sanctified and holy persons for whom we still continue to thank God. 'Take time to be holy' – 'If ye know these things, happy are ye if ye do them' (Jn 13:17).

2

'Mortify, therefore ...'

Sanctify them through thy truth: thy word is truth (John 17:17).

In the last chapter we saw how we need constantly to remind ourselves that the great doctrines of the truth apply to us and we ended by saying that this led to certain inevitable deductions. Now that is what the apostle Paul is always concerned about in all his epistles. For instance, in Romans 6, where he is writing about a very practical question – 'Shall we continue in sin, that grace may abound?' – Paul is really concerned about ordinary daily life and living, and his argument is that people who realise the truth about themselves in Christ will of necessity have a new view of sin. Sin will become something hateful to them, something abhorrent, something which is quite incompatible with their Christian position and their Christian relationships. They will come to regard it as something which is quite profitless. 'What fruit had ye then,' Paul asks, 'in those things whereof ye are now ashamed? for the end of those things is death' (Rom 6:21). That is the argument which you find running through the Bible everywhere, and sin is, therefore, something which the Christian must renounce completely.

So now we come again to the practical application even of that, because there is always the danger that we shall be content with a theoretical understanding, and the Scripture does not allow us to stop at that. We are sanctified by the truth, and through the truth in this way. Therefore, this truth does not merely lay down general principles for us, but it shows our life, and emphasises the all-importance of applying the truth. So if someone comes to us and says, 'I accept all that, but what do I do in practice?' the Scriptures give us our answer, and show us how we are indeed to realise these things in our ordinary daily life.

I wonder whether it has struck us, as it should have done, what a tremendous space is given in the New Testament, in the Gospels and in the epistles, to this ethical teaching, to these very practical matters of daily life and living? It is indeed astonishing to notice this, and especially to notice the detailed character of the teaching. The New Testament never leaves us with generalities; it is never satisfied with laying down principles only. The Bible knows us so well, if I may put it that way. The men who wrote the Gospels under the leading of the Spirit understood both themselves and us so well that they knew that it is never enough merely to state the truth; it has to be applied. Of course, we do not like the application, because when truth is applied it begins to hurt. We like to listen to great pictures of the truth which never become personal; but whether we like it or not, the Scriptures do apply it. They come down, as I shall show you, to the smallest details of life and of living, so that we cannot sit back and just look at this great display of truth which we have here and say, 'That is marvellous,' and then go out and do something which contradicts it all. No, on the contrary, Scripture says everywhere, in the words of our Lord, 'If ye know these things, happy are ye if ye do them' (Jn 13:17). And they are there in order that we may do them and put them into practice. Now I do not know what your impression is, but I sometimes think that this aspect of truth – this detailed application – has been strangely neglected among us; and I wonder whether this has not been partly due to the fact that the tendency of much holiness teaching has been to talk about nothing but surrender. It is said that all you have to do is to surrender yourself, and to be willing to surrender yourself; as if, having done that, you have done everything. But the Scriptures do not teach that. Rather, they bring us down to details and insist upon our applying the truth. Certainly, we surrender ourselves, but we are to surrender ourselves in actual detail and practice all along the line. I think that the results of our failure to remember this detailed ethical teaching, of the epistles in particular, are obvious among us, very often in a failure in things which are quite elemental; and we are not truly evangelical until we are evangelical in our conduct as well as in our belief.

Let us therefore consider how this practical application of the truth, and of the doctrine, is worked out in the Scriptures themselves, and as we do so, let us hold in our minds the order in which the Bible puts it. 'Sanctify them through thy truth' – yes, first and foremost we must be quite clear about the way of salvation, about our position in Christ, and Christ in us. We must start with this great basic doctrine, for if we do not do that, we shall go entirely astray. To start with the principles of daily life and living before considering the doctrines is a complete error, that is to be outside Christ altogether. Indeed, that is the whole error of Roman Catholic teaching, which tends to give the impression that you become a Christian by following a certain ethical practice. But that is to reverse the scriptural order. No, we must start with the great truth, we must see our position, and it is only after we have seen our position in Christ that we begin to say, 'So, then, how do I live it out?' You will find that every New Testament epistle starts with doctrine and then goes on to apply it. Having laid down the doctrine, it says, 'Therefore,' and so we too must put these things in the order in which we are given them. Then, having laid down our doctrine, we come to the application with regard to our conduct.

What, then, is the teaching? Well I think it can be conveniently divided in the way that Scripture commonly does it, in a two-fold manner: it tells us to 'put off the old man' and to 'put on the new man'. You notice the practical way in which it talks. 'Put off the old man' – because of what is true of you, because you are a new man, because you are in Christ and Christ is in you, put off the old man and put on the new.

'I see that,' says someone, 'but what do you mean by putting off the old man? I want to know what that means in daily practice.'

The first answer to that question is that it is another way of saying the words that we have already considered together: 'Reckon ye also yourselves to be dead indeed unto sin, but alive unto God.' When you 'put off the old man', you reckon yourselves to be dead unto sin. When you 'put on the new man', you reckon yourselves to be alive unto God in Jesus Christ and through him.

'Very well, but,' again someone may ask, 'what do you mean by saying I should reckon myself to be dead unto sin?' And so here we come to the details. Reckoning myself to be dead unto sin means, first of all, that there are certain things that I must stop doing. Whatever view we may hold of sanctification and holiness, I can very easily demonstrate to you that the Scriptures come to us and just tell us quite simply and plainly that we must stop doing certain things. For instance, Paul says to Timothy, 'Flee also youthful lusts' (2 Tim 2:22); he does not tell him to spend his time praying about them, he tells him to flee from them!

Let me give you some other examples: 'Let him that stole steal no more' (Eph 4:28); and then we have many examples in the epistle to Titus, where Paul says that the aged women are not to be false accusers and not given to much wine, but teachers of good things; the young women are 'to be discreet, chaste, keepers at home' – not to gad about, as it were, but to realise that they are meant to spend most of their time at home doing the things which they should be doing as wives. Servants, likewise, are not to be guilty of purloining, they are not to answer back (Tit 2:3–10). It is all very detailed. And it does not matter where you turn in the epistles, you will find exactly the same kind of exhortation. You will find that as Christians we are told not to be guilty of foolish talking and jesting, but rather to 'walk in love, as Christ also hath loved us, and hath given himself for us as an offering and a sacrifice to God' (Eph 5:2). Paul says in Ephesians 5:3–4 – and he is writing to Christians, remember – 'But fornication, and all uncleanness or covetousness, let it not be once named among you, as becometh saints. Neither filthiness, nor foolish talking nor jesting, which are not convenient: but rather giving of thanks.' We are just not to do such things. We are not to wait for a special experience of sanctification, we are not to spend the whole of our time in praying; we are just not to do them. We are not to get drunk, we are not to speak evil of one another, and we are not to be guilty of all the other things which the Apostle lists in Ephesians 5.

Surely nothing can be plainer than that. It is the truth which sanctifies, which tells us simply and plainly that we are not to do such things because they are sinful. And we are exhorted as Christian people to break ourselves of such conduct. It may be that we have developed a habit of doing some of these things. We are all guilty of a number of sins of the flesh and of the spirit, and the Scripture says you must break that habit because you are a Christian; you must not do it. Paul speaks in this way to the members of the churches to whom he writes, and he urges a pastor like Titus constantly to remind the people of this: '... these things I will that thou affirm constantly, that they which have believed in God might be careful to maintain good works' (Tit 2:8). He tells them, and Timothy too, that they must cease from these sinful, unworthy habits and practices. It is very difficult to know how to put this plainly, because people often come to me and talk about the great struggle that they are having, and as I listen to them I feel that their real need is just to read the New Testament epistles.

But Paul does not stop at that; that is to do with our actions, the first step in the building. But he goes beyond that and says that we are also to avoid certain things in general. This is an essential part of New Testament teaching at this point. There are certain things that are just not compatible with the Christian life. Now when I say 'things', I do not now mean individual actions, but certain patterns of behaviour which are not compatible with the Christian life and position; the New Testament tells us that we are to avoid all such as a principle and in general.

Let me explain. The apostle John says, 'Love not the world, neither the things that are in the world' (Jn 2:15). The world stands for a certain type and pattern of behaviour, and as Christians (as we have already seen in our great fundamental principles) we no longer belong to the world. We are dead to the world through our union with Christ. When he died, we died, so we glory in the cross of our Lord Jesus Christ 'by whom the world is crucified unto me, and I unto the world' (Gal 6:14). So it is a perfectly fair argument that we are not to love the world, nor the things of the world. Of course, we must remember what worldliness means. We agree that it does not mean some two or three sins which we have long since given up; it is an outlook and mentality, it is 'the lust of the flesh, and the lust of the eyes, and the pride of life' (Jn 2:16). People can be guilty of these things who never darken the door of a theatre or a cinema. This astounding pride which is based upon the flesh, upon what is natural and human – that is the essence of the pride of life and we are not to be guilty of that. Rather, we are to finish with it, however it may manifest itself, and it has many ways of doing so: pride of appearance, pride in clothing or pride in ancestry and all such things. We no longer belong to them, and we must not conform to their pattern in any way whatsoever – love not the world.

Peter puts it like this: '... the time past of our life may suffice us to have wrought the will of the Gentiles' (1 Pet 4:13) – there is a kind of life which is the opposite to that of the Christian. 'You want to continue with that sort of thing,' says Peter in effect, 'but surely you must see that you have already spent enough time out of your life on all that; leave it alone, you do not belong to it.' Or again, as Paul says, 'Ye have not so learned Christ' (Eph 4:20). Read the epistles for yourselves; read Paul again in Ephesians 4: 'This I say therefore, and testify in the Lord, that ye henceforth walk not as other Gentiles walk, in the vanity of their mind' (v. 17). You are no longer to go on doing that, says Paul, you are to be 'renewed in the spirit of your mind' (v. 23): 'Wherefore putting away lying, speak every man truth with his neighbour: for we are members one of another. Be ye angry, and sin not: let not the sun go down upon your wrath: neither give place to the devil. Let him that stole steal no more: but rather let him labour, working with his hands the thing which is good, that he may have to give to him that needeth. Let no corrupt communication proceed out of your mouth, but that which is good to the use of edifying, that it may minister grace unto the hearers' (vv. 25–29).

Now this is the pattern of behaviour to which we are to pay attention, because the truth of God which sanctifies tells us that we no longer belong to the old realm. Or again, the Apostle puts it quite explicitly in 2 Corinthians 6:17 where he says, 'Come out from among them and be ye separate.' Come out from among these people who are not Christian, in your conduct, in your attitude towards life, in the things you enjoy and in the things you read. It may seem narrow, and I agree that it is. But the Christian way of life is narrow, it is the narrowness of the Son of God himself who walked through this world without becoming contaminated by it. We are to separate ourselves from the way which is characteristically worldly. Again, Paul puts this in the form of a great principle – I am simply taking certain characteristic statements at random in order to show you the principles – when he says, 'Make not provision for the flesh' (Rom 13:14). I wonder whether we grasp the meaning of that? Never do anything which you know perfectly well is going to be the means of temptation to you. If you know that certain things, which may not be bad in and of themselves, generally get you down and you are a worse person afterwards than you were before, do not do them; never, as it were, provide yourself with the occasion to sin.

It is amazing how often we do that. I suggest that every time you take up a newspaper you should bear in mind that particular exhortation: 'Make not provision for the flesh.' You see a heading in the newspaper, something in you wants to read it, but something else within you says, 'No!' You know if you read that, it will not do you any good. If you do not read it, you will not lack anything. If you do not know the latest details about the latest sensational murder, it cannot affect your life in any way. If in fact you did not see a newspaper at all, it would not make any real difference. But you are sitting with your newspaper before you and something within you lusts to read it, and if you read it, you know you will not be quite as chaste and pure at the end as you were at the beginning. So by reading that, you have made provision for the flesh and we are told we are not to do so. There are certain things we must not do because we know of their effects. 'Make not provision for the flesh' is the great principle, and because of it we must recognise that certain things are incompatible with our Christian life, and we must just finish with them.

May I enforce all this by telling you a very simple anecdote within my own experience? I do so because I think it not only illustrates my point, but it just shows what the Spirit of God does when he is given free play in a man's life. I refer to a man whom I saw converted to Christ and to the gospel out of, I think I can say without any fear of exaggeration, the most degraded condition in which I have ever seen a man. He lived such a life of sin that he could not read or write. He lived a life of drunkenness and debauchery, but there was one odd thing about this man – in a sense it was laughable and yet it shows what sin can do – he took a particular pride in his moustache. He cultivated this moustache and was very proud of its length. People who knew him assured me that many a time in a state of semi-drunkenness he had fought with men because they had said something about it. Now we may laugh at that, but I could show you things in the life of some polite people which are equally ridiculous.

But this man was converted. Some six weeks after his conversion he came to a mid-week meeting and I noticed to my amazement that he had completely shaved off the moustache. I immediately came to the conclusion that some busybody – perhaps a member of the church – had told him to do so. There was certainly, from my standpoint and from the Christian standpoint, something very ridiculous about this wonderful moustache, and I feared at once that somebody had taken it upon himself to speak to this good man, this lovable character, and had told him to do something about it. So I asked him to remain behind as I wanted to speak to him.

When we were alone, I asked him, 'Who told you to shave

off your moustache?'

'Nobody,' he replied.

But I pressed him because I was curious to know who had made him do it. But he repeated that nobody had told him to shave off his moustache, and I had to believe him.

'All right,' I said, 'if nobody has told you, why have you got rid of it?'

'I will tell you,' he said. 'I got up this morning and after I had washed, I was brushing my hair and I happened to notice myself in the mirror, and I said, as I looked at myself, "That moustache doesn't belong to a Christian!"'

So he had shaved it off. That is it! That is how the truth sanctifies. The man realised that this sort of thing belonged to his old life, and had nothing to do with the new life, though it was the thing of which he was so proud, and for which he had fought and suffered – and he just got rid of it. It is a simple story, but to me it is a very profound one. In the same way, you and I must realise that there are certain things which are not compatible with the life of someone who is in Christ and in whom Christ dwells, and we are bound to have nothing to do with them.

The third step in putting off the old man or reckoning ourselves to be dead unto sin is what has generally been given the scriptural term of 'mortification'; the apostle Paul, for example, says, 'Mortify therefore your members which are upon the earth' (Col 3:5). Now let us hold firmly to the development of the argument. You stop doing certain things and then you go beyond that to the topmost rung of the ladder, and you 'mortify your members'. Let me give you some of the scriptural terms. The apostle James says, 'Cleanse your hands, ye sinners; and purify your hearts, ye double-minded. Be afflicted, and mourn, and weep ...' (Jas 4:8-9). Now certain types of holiness teaching tell us that we are not to mourn and weep, but all we have to do is surrender ourselves and be completely happy. But James exhorts us to grieve because of our sinfulness.

Or again, Paul writes to the Corinthians, 'Having therefore these promises, dearly beloved ...' – and the promises are the doctrines we have already been considering – 'let us cleanse ourselves from all filthiness of the flesh and spirit, perfecting holiness in the fear of God' (2 Cor 7:1). I am told that I must cleanse myself. When Paul tells me that I must mortify my members which are on the earth, he gives a list of what he means by that, and tells me how I am to do it. Then in Romans 8:13 he says, 'If ye through the Spirit do mortify the deeds of the body, ye shall live.' Again, take his great statement in 1 Corinthians 9:27 where, referring to himself as a preacher, he says, 'I keep under my body.'

Now all this is just the scriptural way of putting before us the doctrine of the mortification of the flesh. Yes, I know about the dangers. I know we are all beginning to think of camel hair shirts and of anchorites and hermits living on a lonely island far away from everybody. That, however, is false asceticism, which the Scripture never teaches. But because we dislike false asceticism, we must not deny the scriptural doctrine of mortification of the flesh, which is something we are all expected to do. This means that we must realise that as a result of sin and the Fall, the very powers and qualities which God has put in us by nature tend to become our enemies; and though we are Christians, the remnants of the old man are still here and we are not perfect. The flesh remains and because of that we are always to be watching the body. 'I keep under my body,' says the Apostle in 1 Corinthians 9:27, for he realised that if he did not, he would go astray.

There is great teaching on that in the New Testament. You will find, for example, that one of the most solemn warnings that our Lord gave to his people was when he warned them of such things as gluttony – excess of eating and drinking. We can indulge the body, not only by committing acts of immorality, but in other respects such as food and drink and sleep, and a general spirit of lethargy, and I must not sin in these things either. I am sure we all know ourselves well enough to understand that the body reacts upon the spirit and the spirit upon the body, and if my body, due to any excess in any respect, is lethargic and dull, if I have not had enough sleep and am over-tired, or if I have slept too much, or done too much – and we are all guilty of these things – then I find it very difficult to read my Bible intelligently. We must not let the body dictate. It is always anxious to do so, and if we listened to the body, we should always be guilty of some excess or other. The Apostle said he kept it under – the original Greek says he pummelled it, or made it black and blue – and he did all this in order to keep it down, because if he did not, he would suffer spiritually.

And so, here we are, confronted by this great teaching about the mortification of the flesh. In other words, we are not only to refrain from certain actions because we know they are sinful, but must also realise that we must actively carry out these scriptural commands in order to keep down the motions of sin which are yet within us, for if we do not, they will get the ascendancy. The thing I am anxious to impress upon you is that all that I am putting before you is a part of the truth by which we are sanctified – 'Sanctify them through thy truth.'

Let me finally deal briefly with the other aspect. There is another side – 'Put on the new man …' 'Reckon yourselves to be alive unto God through Jesus Christ.' This is another way of saying, you must think all this out in practice; you must remind yourself of who you are; 'Work out your own salvation with fear and trembling …' Why? '… For it is God which worketh in you …' (Phil 2:12-13). Those were our first great principles. Because God is 'working in you both to will and to do', you 'work it out with fear and trembling'. Because you are who you are and what you are, '… follow after righteousness, godliness, faith, love, patience, meekness. Fight the good fight of faith, and lay hold of eternal life' (1 Tim 6:11-12). You and I are exhorted to do these things – to follow after, to lay hold upon them. '… giving all diligence,' says Peter, 'add to your faith' – furnish it with – 'virtue; and to virtue knowledge; and to knowledge temperance; and to temperance patience; and to patience godliness; and to godliness brotherly kindness; and to brotherly kindness charity' (2 Pet 1:5-7). And as you read on in 2 Peter chapter 1, you will find he tells us that the man who does not do these things is blind and cannot see afar off; he does not realise that he has been purged from his own sins; but the man who does these things is making his calling and election sure. We must 'put on the new man' and do all these things. A further great illustration of this is in the epistle to Titus, where the Apostle tells Titus that he must exhort these people to be 'careful to maintain good works' (Tit 3:8).

We must leave it at that now, though we shall have to return to it again, but I was anxious that we should see the two sides and that we should work them out in detail – put off, put on; reckon yourselves to be dead, reckon yourselves to be alive.

All this is addressed to us, and it is something which we are called upon to do. It is as we thus obey these exhortations and the things of the Spirit, that we find ourselves becoming sanctified. Do not forget the order in which I put this truth to you. We must always start by saying that sanctification is God's work in us. It is a prayer to God – 'Sanctify them through thy truth' – it is God who does it, but he does it by giving us the truth, and by giving us the Holy Spirit who enables us to understand the truth and apply it. The work of the Spirit is to bring us into this relationship to the truth by opening our eyes to it, by giving us a desire to practise it and by enabling us to do so; but he sanctifies us through the truth. Let us never forget these details. Let us never argue about certain things or wait to have some big experience before we stop doing all these wrong things. No, we are told immediately: Stop doing it, avoid all that type of behaviour. Remember and realise the danger and therefore constantly mortify the flesh and keep under the body. May God in his infinite grace and kindness enable us to receive such teaching and practise it day by day.

3

Spiritually Well Dressed

Sanctify them through thy truth: thy word is truth (John 17:17).

As we continue with this great petition which our Lord offered for his immediate followers, and for his followers at all times, it is good for us to remind ourselves again that the ultimate end and object of our salvation is that we should be able to stand in the presence of God. That is the only right way of considering our salvation. Salvation is not just a question of being forgiven; that is essential, of course, and the first essential, but it is only the negative aspect. The wonderful thing about our salvation is that we are promised that we shall finally stand faultless and blameless, without spot and without rebuke, in the presence of God. That is the blessed hope that is set before us, and therefore Scripture argues in so many places that '… every man that hath this hope in him purifieth himself, even as he is pure' (1 Jn 3:3).

So as I understand this New Testament teaching, holiness is not something about which we should make appeals to people. It is our business to set scriptural doctrine before them, and the man who really believes what he claims to believe is a man who must be urgently concerned about this question of his sanctification. If this doctrine of sanctification is unimportant to anyone, then such a person is just confessing that he or she is not a Christian. If we really believe that we are going on to stand in the presence of God and of Christ, there is no time to be lost, and the most urgent problem before us is, therefore, to learn how this sanctification of ours takes place; and that has been our immediate theme. We have seen that God sanctifies us through the truth, through the great doctrines, and we have shown from Scripture how these must be applied in our lives.

In our last study we were considering the negative aspect of this application, and now we come to the positive. Having put off that which was characteristic of the old man, and having reckoned ourselves to be dead unto sin, we are now reckoning ourselves, regarding ourselves, as Christians, to be alive unto God – we are looking at positive holiness, the positive living of the godly life. Now it seems to me that one of the most convenient ways of considering this positive emphasis and this aspect of the doctrine is to study the message of Colossians 3 which is a perfect statement of this truth, although, of course, parallel statements are to be found elsewhere, in Ephesians, for instance. Indeed, you find this teaching in every single New Testament epistle, for all the epistles are concerned about holiness; they are written to Christians and their one object is to get these people to know who they are and to live accordingly.

Let us look, then, at Colossians 3 in order that we may see how the Apostle develops his argument. To me there is nothing more fascinating than to observe the way in which Paul states this great truth in different ways. It is ever the one message, but he puts it in different forms. Here in Colossians he starts with his doctrine: 'If ye then be risen with Christ ...' Well, how do you know that that is true of you? That is where the doctrine comes in; the fact is that you are in Christ, that you are united to him, and therefore everything that has happened to Christ has happened to you. You have died with him, you have been crucified, you are buried with him, yes, but you have also risen with him, and so, 'If ye then be risen with Christ, seek those things which are above, where Christ sitteth on the right hand of God.' 'Set your affection,' says Paul, 'on things above, not on things on the earth.' Why? 'For ye are dead, and your life is hid with Christ in God. When Christ, who is our life, shall appear, then shall ye also appear with him in glory.'

What a marvellous summary of those great items of doctrine

which we have considered one by one! I have had to mention them again because you will always find that the Apostle never deals with any detailed, or any small problem without putting it into the context of the truth and of the doctrine, and that is one of the most important things we can ever remember. That is, as I have often pointed out, the whole tragedy of the Roman Catholic conception of holiness, for, with all its detailed information, it so often loses the connection. The sanctified life becomes an end in and of itself. But that is never scriptural. It is because of certain things that we do other things. We do not do them in order to be Christian, we do them *because* we are Christian. 'If ye be risen with Christ ...' and so on – it is the same idea as 'reckoning ourselves'. 'Set your affection on things above' – think on these things which are above, and seek them.

We should start every day of our lives, let me emphasise this again, by saying to ourselves, 'I am a child of God, I died with Christ, I am dead unto sin, I am risen with Christ, I am in this new realm.' *Therefore*, 'Set your affections', seek these things, which must ever be first and foremost and uppermost in our minds, and in our whole outlook. Remember, too, that this is an exhortation, it is a command, and I must do it. I do not just wait until a feeling possesses me and makes me do it. No, I have to seek these things, and set my affections on things above. I must be doing it myself. Then, having said that, as we saw earlier, Paul brings in his negative – 'Mortify therefore your members that are on the earth.'

But now we are interested in the positive side to all this, which begins at verse 12. Again I pause to make the point clear, that I have no right to start here unless I have previously grasped the doctrine of the eleven verses that go before it. But having done that, I now come on to the message of verse 12, and here again there are certain words which we must stress, because, once more, they emphasise our activity. To grow in grace, and to become ever increasingly sanctified, calls upon us to do certain things. It is not just a question of surrender and looking to the Lord. No, I am commanded to do certain things, and here they are. The characteristic terms come out once more, so let me note them before we come to look at them in detail. I have to 'put on', and I have to 'let' certain things – 'let the peace of God rule in your hearts'. I am told, indeed, to be 'thankful' and told that everything I do must be done 'in the name of the Lord': '... whatsoever ye do in word or deed, do all in the name of the Lord Jesus, giving thanks unto God and the Father by him' (3:17).

I think, therefore, that the principle which we have already laid down is once more illustrated here very abundantly, namely, that you and I are told to put these things into practice; God's commands are positive, as well as negative. We can divide this positive teaching into two main sections. First of all, Paul gives certain general principles in connection with this godly, holy, sanctified life, and then he goes on to his detailed application. It is the method of division that the Apostle always employs: realise your character, develop it and then work it out in detail. He does not start with the details, but with the character and disposition. What is it, then, this disposition that the Christian has always to be bearing in mind and always to be developing and nurturing?

The first exhortation is in verse 12: 'Put on therefore as the elect of God', and the picture, clearly, is of putting on certain items of clothing. It is, of course, an illustration and we must be careful not to press the illustration too far. It does not mean, obviously, that the Christian just puts on a certain kind of behaviour while he himself is something apart from that which he puts on. No, when Paul says 'put on', he means not only *look* like this but *be* like this. It is a good illustration, and the Apostle is very fond of it. Take, for instance, how he uses the same picture in writing to the Philippians, to whom he says, 'Only let your conversation be as becometh the gospel of Christ' (Phil 1:27). He is thinking in terms of clothing, and he says, in effect, 'Now think of yourself putting on certain apparel, let it be becoming, let it be consistent with your complexion and figure. There must be no clashing of colour and style, everything must harmonise and go together.' Then in his exhortation to Titus, the Apostle talks about 'adorning the doctrine' (Tit 2:10). In other words, you can think of the doctrine as a man's suit, or clothing, and our conduct and mien as a kind of adornment which adds the finishing touches.

Now that is the idea which Paul has here in Colossians 3:12, but, again, as a wise teacher he knows that it is not enough just to make a general statement. He goes on to particulars: 'Put on therefore, as the elect of God, holy and beloved, bowels of mercies, kindness ...' – these things need no explanation, I know. What I want to emphasise is that you and I are *told* to be kind; the teaching of sanctification is not one that tells you just to wait and hope that something is going to happen to you, a great experience which will make you kind. Not at all! If you want the big experience, be kind. You will get it by being kind. Nobody can be kind for us, it is something we must do ourselves. Then the next characteristic which Paul refers to is humbleness of mind, which means humility, and this, too, is something we must develop in ourselves. None of us are humble-minded by nature. We are all aggressive and assertive. Some show it in different ways from others, but it is true of all of us, and if we are to be truly humble, it will mean watching and controlling ourselves: humility is something that you and I are to 'put on'.

Then there is meekness. It would be good to consider all these words one by one slowly, but I am trying to give a composite picture here. However, for your own interest, work out the difference between humility and meekness and you will see that it is very significant. Next we have longsuffering – being patient with one another. It is very difficult, as we all know, to be patient with certain people, it is not easy to be longsuffering, and yet if we are to be sanctified, we must take ourselves in hand and develop this part of the Christian character. If you claim to be born with an impatient temperament, then you must control it. You are given strength and power to do this, but it is you who have to do it.

We must put all these things into practice. It is something which you and I must do day by day, hour by hour, and minute by minute. We start well in the morning, then something happens and at that moment we must watch and remember and develop this character; and the more we develop it, the more we are unlikely to fail in detail at odd moments.

Then in verse 13 Paul says, '... forgiving one another, if any man have a quarrel against any: even as Christ forgave you, so also do ye.' This again is something we just have to do. A person has wronged us. Very well, we do not turn our backs and pass that person without looking at him or her – not at all! We must face this matter and reason with ourselves about it in terms of the gospel. We must say to ourselves, 'God forgave me in Christ, he even sent Christ to the cross in order that I might be forgiven, though I repeatedly insulted him and deliberately sinned against him. If God has done that for me, I must forgive this person, come what may.' We make ourselves do it. That is the New Testament teaching on sanctification.

And then another most interesting way of applying the truth is given in verse 14: 'Above all these things put on charity [love] which is the bond of perfectness.' This is an interesting picture. 'Above all these things' really means over or upon all these things. You notice what Paul is doing. We have, as it were, been putting on item after item of clothing, and having done that, we hold them all in position by putting on this garment of perfectness which is love. All these different items must be held together by this wonderful cloak, which binds everything together in perfect harmony, and presents a complete and perfect and unified picture.

Now that is the first great exhortation. We are to put on all this, and you see how it illustrates perfectly those words to which I have already referred, that line in the hymn which tells us to 'Take time to be holy.' Take time to dress yourself spiritually, do not dress in a hurry every morning. And notice, too, that the tense is present. We do not just put these things on once, and think that we are dressed for the rest of our lives. On the contrary, we are to keep on doing it. How true that is in our own experience! Take time to dress spiritually in the morning, and then throughout the day check that everything is in position, look regularly at yourself in the mirror, as it were. Take time to be holy.

Paul's next general exhortation is in verse 15. He says, 'Let the peace of God rule in your hearts, to the which also ye are called in one body; and be ye thankful.' That is again a wonderful thing. Another way of translating it would be, 'Let the peace of God act as an umpire in your hearts ...' It is the peace that Christ gave to his disciples just before he died: 'Peace I leave with you, my peace I give unto you' (Jn 14:27). Well, says the Apostle, see that it rules among you. If you feel you are hurt, take it to the umpire. Do not decide for yourself, or say, 'This is my right.' Let the peace of God act as an umpire – the peace of Christ both in your own heart, and also among you. You are called into one body, so let nothing disrupt the peace of Christ. Then, as you learn to take difficulties to the umpire, you will be growing in sanctification.

The last exhortation in that verse is, 'Be ye thankful.' We tend to think of thankfulness as a feeling, but the Apostle commands us to be thankful, whether we feel like it or not. We must, he says, keep on becoming thankful – that is another way of translating it. 'But if it is not a feeling,' says someone, 'what is it?' Again, a well known hymn puts it perfectly, when it says:

> Count your blessings, name them one by one
> And it will surprise you what the Lord hath done.

But suppose you wake up in the morning and do not feel at all thankful. In fact, suppose you feel the reverse, so that though the Apostle says, 'Be ye thankful,' you answer, 'I cannot honestly say I feel that way.' How, then, can you make yourself thankful? You do it by just waiting for a moment and considering. You count your blessings; you just go back over your life and list the things that have happened to you. Why are you a Christian at all? Why are you forgiven at all? What has your story been? Have goodness and mercy followed you? Go back over it all. Yes, count your blessings, name them one by one, and if you do this, it will surprise you what the Lord has done. If you take the trouble, you will find yourself thankful.

And the next word for us is. 'Let the word of Christ dwell in you richly in all wisdom; teaching and admonishing one another in psalms and hymns and spiritual songs, singing with grace in your hearts to the Lord.' Again, notice the command. The word of Christ, the word that Christ himself taught, *must* dwell in us richly. 'But how do I let it dwell in me richly?' you ask. We do that by reading it, by meditating upon it, and by talking to other people about it. We must soak ourselves in it, for we can never read it too much. The more we read it, the more it will be in us. And as we are keeping and controlling all this, as we are letting it dwell in us, we shall have a marvellous life, we shall enjoy ourselves all together; and at the same time we shall be demonstrating to the world God's handiwork in us as Christian people.

And then, lastly, Paul sums it all up by saying, 'And whatsoever ye do in word or deed, do all in the name of the Lord Jesus, giving thanks to God and the Father by him.' Do it all, in other words, in the spirit of Christ himself. Not only are we to do these things, but the way in which we do them is so important: 'Do all in the name of the Lord Jesus.' Do it in the way he did it. Again, I could illustrate almost endlessly. You remember how Paul, in taking up the collection of the church at Corinth, tells us how to put our contribution on the plate? We must be wholehearted givers, we must give happily, not grudgingly with a sort of hesitancy – no! God loves the cheerful giver (2 Cor 9:7). So we must do all things like this. As he gave himself, let us do these things; let us put on these articles of clothing with cheerfulness in the spirit of Christ. Let us not regard them as a kind of straightjacket, but as the most beautiful robe the world has ever seen – we must do it as Christ did it.

There, then, are the general principles. But we must look briefly at the details, which Paul now goes on to apply from verse 18. Scripture never stops at general principles, it always goes on to the details, and Paul does that here. For example, 'Wives, submit yourselves unto your own husbands, as it is fit in the Lord.' As he puts it in Ephesians 5:23: 'The husband is the head of the wife, even as Christ is the head of the church' – that is Christian doctrine – is it being remembered and observed today? I must point out again that there are evangelical people who seem to me constantly to ignore the plain teaching of the word of God, because it does not tally with modern ideas. But that is the teaching of the Scriptures. But then, you notice, Paul says to husbands, '… love your wives, and be not bitter against them.' You can see that in every one of these exhortations the Apostle seems to put his finger directly on the thing which is most dangerous – it is clear both in the case of the wife, and of the husband. The peculiar temptation of the husband is to be bitter against his wife, to look down upon her, perhaps to despise her in certain ways, to regard her as someone who is meant to serve him. He is the head, he is put into that position, but he must not lord it over his wife in any spirit of bitterness.

Then we come to the children: 'Children, obey your parents in all things: for this is well pleasing unto the Lord' (v. 20). How this doctrine is needed today. Even among Christian people discipline seems to have vanished. But then you notice that there follows a wonderful and glorious appeal: 'Fathers, provoke not your children to anger lest they be discouraged.' Compare our age with the Victorian age. The bitterness or the lack of discipline among children is obvious today, but this exhortation to the fathers does not seem to be needed so much in these days as it was by the typical Victorian father. But in a sense it is always needed. We must always observe this appeal, because if the children are to obey their parents, the parents are not to be unreasonable with the children, they are not to provoke them lest they be discouraged. Parents are not merely to say, 'Because I say so – therefore you have to do it.' No, give reasons to your children as far as you can, let your command be made reasonably. Do not discourage them, says the Apostle.

And then he comes to the servants: 'Servants, obey in all things your masters … not with eyeservice, as menpleasers; but in singleness of heart, fearing God.' Be careful you do this in the right way; and again, 'Whatsoever ye do, do it heartily as unto the Lord and not unto men' (v. 23). That applies to the husband, to the wife, to the children, to the parents, to the masters and to the servants. We must not just say, 'I suppose as a Christian I ought to' – that is not the way to do it. Do it gladly and heartily *because* you are a Christian. Rejoice that you are given such a high standard, and that you are privileged to do so. But then Paul goes on still further in the fourth chapter and says, 'Masters, give unto your servants that which is just and equal; knowing that ye also have a Master in heaven.' We still need to be reminded of that. There are people who would say that the church is as she is today because so often our fathers and our forefathers forgot this detailed injunction. They might be in church on a Sunday morning but some poor slave was staying at home to cook the dinner. No, this is the Christian injunction and the injunction was not only to the servants, it was also to the masters. It is universal: we are all Christians together.

And then Paul talks about prayer, and about the way in which we are to speak. Our speech must be with grace, seasoned with salt, because there are others watching us who are interested in our conduct and our behaviour.

You see, therefore, how the Apostle has not only taken us through the principles, but has also applied them in detail. I would again emphasise this all-important general point that covers everything – it is you and I who are called upon to do these things. This is God's way of sanctification; this is the way we put on the new man, and the way in which we reckon ourselves to be alive unto God. I must examine myself; it is not merely what I feel in church services, but how I have been living. How am I behaving as a husband or father? How am I behaving as a master? How am I behaving in all these relationships in life? Have I lost my temper? Have I become irritable? How have I behaved as a Christian? Some of the greatest saints throughout the ages, men like John Fletcher of Madeley, asked themselves such questions at the end of every day, and we, too, must examine our lives in detail. We have no right not to do so; we must implement these detailed exhortations. We must take these things one by one, and it is only as we do so that we become sanctified through the truth, in the truth, by the truth. Here is the truth, the word of God himself, and it is as this word comes to me in the power of the Spirit, and as I give obedience to it and apply it, and put it into practice, that I shall find that I

am being given strength to obey. So, 'work out your own salvation' – it is you who must do it – 'in fear and trembling. For
it is God which worketh in you both to will and to do ...' (Phil
2:13). And it happens like this. As I read this word, God creates
within me a desire to be like that. He makes me long to be like
that, and as I am desiring it, I try to put it into practice, and I find
that he gives me strength: 'both to will and to do...' So you need
not wait for power; as you do these things you will be given it.
God gives the power to people who want to be like this. As you
are making your effort you will find this strength, for he
empowers you by the Holy Spirit.

So there it is. We have hurried through it in order that we may
have a composite picture and see the method, and now we go
out to live this kind of life in detail. You and I are to be such that
as we walk up and down the streets of life, people will be struck
and attracted. You have seen them turn and look at a well-dres-
sed person. Well, it is something like that. They should be
struck by us, and look at us, and think, 'What is this person? I
have never seen anybody quite like this before! What perfection!
What balance! How everything fits together! How graceful!'
That is the kind of people we can be and the kind of people that
we must be. And when we become such people, believe me, the
revival we are longing for will start, and the people outside, in
their misery and wretchedness, will come in and will want to
know about it.

O may God enlighten us and give us understanding concerning this plain, simple, direct teaching, and above all enable us to
put it into practice. Then, when the day comes for us to stand
before him, let us be ready, always 'well dressed', always clean,
always ready to be ushered into his glorious presence.

4

The Work of the Holy Spirit

But the Comforter, which is the Holy Ghost, whom the Father will send in my name, he shall teach you all things and bring all things to your remembrance, whatsoever I have said unto you (John 14:26).

This verse introduces us at once to the essential teaching in the New Testament concerning the work and Person of the Holy Spirit, and we must consider it in the context of John 17:17, where our Lord prays, 'Sanctify them through thy truth: thy word is truth.' We have been engaged in a consideration of this whole question of our sanctification; and of the various aspects of the truth from which our sanctification is produced and is promoted. And, of course, in considering this great comprehensive truth, we come, of necessity, to the truth concerning the Holy Spirit, his Person and his work. This is an essential part of the message of salvation and it is, therefore, an integral part of the doctrine concerning our sanctification. There is no doubt at all but that that is why our Lord specifically introduces this particular teaching at this particular point. From chapter 14 right into chapter 17 of John's Gospel you will find our Lord's most explicit teaching concerning the Person and the work of the Holy Spirit, and it is not surprising that he should have done so at that precise juncture.

Here he is, about to leave them. He has already told them that he is about to go from them; he has said to Peter, 'Whither I go, thou canst not follow me now; but thou shalt follow me after-wards' (Jn 13:36); and the effect of that is that the disciples' hearts are troubled. That is why our Lord begins this wonderful pas-sage by saying to them, 'Let not your heart be troubled: ye believe in God, believe also in me' (Jn 14:1), and that in turn leads on to this doctrine of the Holy Spirit. 'If you love me,' he says in verses 15 to 18, 'keep my commandments. And I will pray the Father, and he shall give you another Comforter, that he may abide with you for ever; even the Spirit of truth; whom the world cannot receive, because it seeth him not, neither knoweth him: but ye know him; for he dwelleth with you, and shall be in you. I will not leave you comfortless: I will come to you.'

Our Lord then elaborates this great teaching on the work of the Holy Spirit and we can summarise it like this. Our Lord tells these men that they must not grieve because of his departure. Indeed, he actually says in chapter 16:7 that it is expedient for them – that it is a good thing for them – that he should be going away, because, he says, 'If I go not away, the Comforter will not come unto you; but if I depart, I will send him unto you.' And that is good because the Comforter is going to take his place, as our Teacher, as our Leader, as our Strengthener, and as the one who stands by us and with us, to help us. He will be our Advocate in that sense, and therefore, clearly, the business of the Holy Spirit is to continue, and, indeed, to increase the work which the Lord himself had begun to do while he was here in the days of his flesh. He says in this same context, 'I have yet many things to say unto you, but ye cannot bear them now. Howbeit when he, the Spirit of truth, is come, he will guide you into all truth …' (Jn 16:12–13).

In other words, while our Lord was yet with them they could not fully understand the significance of his Person, neither could they understand the purpose of his death, and they stumbled at it. But afterwards, after the death and the Resurrection, when the Holy Spirit came, he would explain and apply these things to them and enable them to reap their wonderful benefits. And so our Lord tells them here about this other Comforter whom he is going to send to them, and we, at the moment, are particularly interested in this from the standpoint of our sanctification. So we will look at the place and the work of the Holy Spirit in our sanctification.

Clearly this is a vital subject for us, and we cannot be too careful in our handling of it. We have seen from the very beginning how our Lord has prayed that God should bring about our sanctification: 'Sanctify them through thy truth,' he prays. Sanctification, basically and ultimately, is the work of God; the whole of our salvation is the work of God, but sanctification is so in particular. It is something that God does to us and in us, and we have seen that he does it by means of the truth. But the doctrine of the Holy Spirit reminds us in particular that it is God's work, and therefore it behoves us to discover how it is done. God does this work in us and upon us through the Holy Spirit, but the question is: how does the Holy Spirit do this? Now I need scarcely remind you that there is a great deal of confusion with regard to this subject. There are devout people in the church who hold different opinions as to the way in which the Holy Spirit works. The doctrine of the Holy Spirit, not surprisingly, has often been used by our adversary the devil to lead people astray, so that we cannot be too careful about this matter.

Therefore it seems to me that we must start with the great basic fact that we must always be careful to draw a sharp distinction between the gifts of the Spirit, and what we may call the graces of the Spirit. The Holy Spirit, it is clearly shown in the New Testament, does two main works. First of all there is what is more or less an external work of witness. Peter, we are told in Acts 5:32, says to the authorities, 'And we are his witnesses of these things; and so is also the Holy Ghost, whom God hath given to them that obey him.' It is quite clear that what happened on the Day of Pentecost in Jerusalem – the events which are recorded in Acts 2 – has reference mainly to this external work of the Spirit. There the Holy Spirit descended upon the church in that particular form, 'cloven tongues like as of fire', and gave them an ability to speak in different tongues in order that this external witness might be borne, and of course we are given references to the same thing elsewhere in the Scriptures.

Therefore, in that connection the work of the Holy Spirit was to draw attention to these men who constituted the Christian church. They were given power and authority, and also different abilities, and by means of these things, as the record shows, they arrested attention. People said, 'What is this? What has happened to these men? They are obviously Galileans, yet we hear them all speaking in our own tongues? What is this phenomenon?' Some even said, 'These men are drunk!' It was obvious that there was something very strange about them, and that attracted attention. As a result the Apostle Peter had liberty to preach the gospel and to present the great facts of salvation. Indeed, as you go through Acts, you will find a similar work done; the Spirit comes in this external form and gives men these abilities in order that they may act as witnesses.

But there is another work of the Spirit, and that is his work specifically in connection with our sanctification: the work that he does within us, the work that he does down in the very depths and recesses of our personalities. Often people do not keep these two things separate; there is confusion between the external and the internal work of the Spirit. People often imagine that the work of the Spirit in sanctification is manifested and demonstrated in terms of gifts, rather than in terms of that which is done deep down in the soul; and it is at that point, I think you will agree, that most of the confusion tends to occur. Therefore, let us start with this great, fundamental distinction. There are gifts of the Spirit and they vary from case to case as Paul teaches us in 1 Corinthians 12, but all that is something different from the work that the Spirit does within us. You remember how Paul, having enumerated these various wonderful gifts, says, 'Yet shew I unto you a more excellent way' (1 Cor 12:31), and the more excellent way is the way that leads to this work of the Spirit within us, producing the fruits of the Spirit and the graces of the Spirit – Paul's great disquisition upon the subject of love. If we hold that in our minds as our basic distinction, it will save us from many troubles.

Having said that, let me still ask the same question – how does the Holy Spirit perform this work of salvation within us, and, especially how does he do this work of our sanctification? Here again I feel it is important for us to start with two negatives – the first is that *we must never regard the doctrine of the Holy Spirit in isolation.* By this I mean that we must always realise that the work of salvation is one. There are various aspects of it, and we must distinguish between them, but there is all the difference in the world between distinguishing them as aspects of salvation, and separating these various aspects into differing entities and parts in and of themselves.

Let us look at it like this. We have been at pains to remind one another that we must never separate justification by faith from sanctification. You can distinguish between them but you must never separate them. What I mean by separating is this: there are people, as we have seen, who will tell you that you can be justified without being sanctified, and then they say that as you have received your justification by faith, you now go on to receive your sanctification by faith. That is patently false teaching because it is pressing the distinction into something that separates. You cannot be justified without the process of sanctification already having been started. From the moment that a man is justified by faith in Christ, his sanctification has commenced; and it is for this reason that you cannot divide the Lord Jesus Christ, who himself is made unto us wisdom, and righteousness – or justification – and sanctification and redemption (1 Cor 1:30). You cannot receive parts of the Lord Jesus Christ; you receive him as a whole, so that Christ who is your justification is already your sanctification. And we must be careful that we do not fall into exactly the same error with regard to this question of the work of the Holy Spirit in our sanctification.

Again, people tend to do it like this: they say, 'O yes, of course, you need to be introduced first to the teaching about the Lord Jesus Christ, and then, if you have received that teaching, you go on to the teaching about the Holy Spirit.' Indeed there are some who would even regard those who make this distinction as unusually spiritual Christians because they do that. They say, 'We are not still interested in the doctrine of the Lord Jesus

Christ; that happened when we were converted.' They have now left that behind them and have gone on further and are now always teaching about the Holy Spirit. But that is very false, unscriptural teaching. The whole work of salvation is the work of the blessed triune God, and the three Persons of the blessed Holy Trinity are always engaged in this work.

If you want to draw a distinction, it is that the eternal Father planned and originated the work; God the Son, the second Person, has actually come into the world and has carried out the work, and it is the special function of the Holy Spirit to apply that work to us. But, obviously, you cannot isolate these three and separate them. You distinguish between them in your mind and thinking, and it is right that you should do so – indeed we must do so. But we must obviously never speak of having now gone on from the doctrine of Christ to the doctrine of the Holy Spirit, because that is a sheer impossibility. You cannot separate the three Persons in the blessed Trinity, they are eternally one. They have divided up the work in this way among themselves as a kind of function, but always, everywhere, we are concerned about them all, and concerned about them all at exactly the same point.

So we must always be careful not to isolate this great doctrine of the Holy Spirit. It must be held together with all the other doctrines. We can look at it in particular but never in the sense of putting it into a compartment by itself and inviting people to go on from there to something else. As we cannot divide the Trinity, so we cannot divide in this fundamental sense the work of the Trinity. The doctrine of the Holy Spirit must be held together with the full doctrine since this is an aspect of the great, wonderful, central doctrine.

My second negative is that *we must not isolate the activity of the Holy Spirit*. You will know that in the history of the church there have been people who have isolated the work of the Holy Spirit from everything else. I speak with considerable admiration of the great George Fox, the founder of the 'Friends' and I can say truthfully that I have never read anything about or by George Fox, without feeling my heart warmed and without feeling that I have derived a blessing. Yet there is no question at all but that at certain points he introduced a teaching which is directly contrary to that of the Scriptures, namely, when he isolated the activity of the Spirit, and put his emphasis upon what he called the 'inner light'.

Now I am in considerable sympathy with him, for he did it, of course, as a reaction. George Fox could see that there were many people who were highly orthodox, who knew their Scriptures from cover to cover, who could recite them and reason about them and argue about them and preach about them – people who knew their doctrine, but it was very clear to George Fox that it was all head knowledge, it was purely intellectual. Indeed when you looked at these people in the context of the New Testament, you could see that they were lacking in life and in spiritual power and spirituality. They were often living worldly lives, indeed, they seemed to be living their life in compartments. To George Fox, these people were formalists who regarded their houses as preaching houses. He did not hesitate to go in and upset their meetings, and he preached in the power of the Spirit. But in reaction to all that dead formality, he went to the other extreme, and said that nothing mattered except that they should listen to the 'inner light' and be guided by it – they should listen to the Spirit within them.

Now George Fox himself had a strong belief in orthodox doctrine, but he taught it in such a way as really to deny it, and the result was that many of his followers have taken up the position of saying that all you have to do is to listen to this Power within you. He taught that the Holy Spirit is in every man and all you have to do is be obedient to this Spirit within you and obey the 'inner light'. He said you do not need anything else, you do not need any external teaching. Those who hold this view tend to contrast the inner light with the teaching of the word of God; they isolate the work and the activity of the Holy Spirit. And of course this is the danger to which we are all subject. Our error is that we tend to isolate, not only the doctrine concerning the Spirit, but even the activity of the Spirit as well.

How, then, do we avoid falling into this error? I suggest to you that we avoid it in the following way. There are two main tests which we must always apply to anything that we feel is the work of the Spirit, or anything that may be represented to us as being the work of the Spirit. The first test is to ask whether we are being directed to the word of God. The New Testament teaches that in the work of sanctification the Holy Spirit works in connection with the word. He does act upon us directly, but almost invariably he does so in connection with the word, the Scripture. This is a very fundamental point. If you read the scriptural teaching concerning the Holy Spirit and his work, if indeed you read in general about the work of sanctification, you will always find that the work of the Spirit and the word go together and that the terms are used interchangeably. Sometimes we are told that we are sanctified by the word; at other times that we are sanctified by the Spirit. Sometimes we are told we are born again and regenerated by the Spirit; at other times we are told we are regenerated by the word. Both James and Peter teach that our regeneration is the result of the word; at other times the emphasis is upon the Spirit. Thus what is clearly meant is that the Spirit does this work in and through us, and upon us, by means of the word – by using the word.

You notice, too, that our Lord describes the Holy Spirit as the Spirit of truth. He is the Spirit who brings and will lead us in to all truth. He is not only the true Spirit, but he is also the Spirit who particularly reveals the truth. That is his greatest function. Our Lord says in John 14:26, 'The Comforter, which is the Holy Ghost, whom the Father will send in my name, he shall teach you all things, and bring all things to your remembrance, whatsoever I have said unto you.' What we have to discover is: how does the Holy Spirit fulfil his great task of revealing the truth? There is no doubt at all about this. The apostle Paul in 1 Corinthians 2:12, a most important verse, says, 'Now we have received, not the spirit of the world, but the spirit which is of God; that we might know the things that are freely given us of God.' That is the difference, says Paul, between the Christian and the non–Christian. The non-Christian does not understand these things of God, he does not understand this question of salvation. The average person of the world today is not interested in salvation at all, nor in his relationship to God. This is because he has not the Spirit, but the Spirit is given that we might know the things that are freely given to us by God.

And what are these things? What are the 'wonderful works of God' referred to in Acts 2:11? How may I know about them; how may I understand them? The answer is that I cannot know anything about them until I come to this book. It is here that I discover them; it is here and here alone that I know what God has done. I may have certain experiences, but the question is, have they anything to do with these wonderful works of God? It is only in the word that I discover what God has done, and it is only here that I can discover what these things are that are freely given to us of God. It is the Spirit who has done it and he has done it by taking hold of certain men and doing two things to them.

He has, first of all, given them a revelation of the truth. He has given information concerning the facts – which is what revelation means. But he has not stopped merely at revelation, he has also inspired them, which means that he has so controlled them that in giving their accounts of these facts, they have been kept free from error. It is the double work. Revelation means a knowledge of the facts of salvation; inspiration means the work of controlling men and guiding them in recording these facts so that they are free from error. And that is what we have in the Scriptures. Prophecy, says Peter in 2 Peter 1:20–21 is not the result of any private interpretation; prophecy did not come in past times because certain men had what they called 'insight' into the events and facts. Not at all! Prophecy is not man putting down on paper what he thinks is happening in the world or what is going to happen; it has not come by any private excogitation in that way. Rather, as Peter puts it, 'Holy men of God spake as they were moved by the Holy Ghost' (2 Pet 1:21). Holy men spoke from God, as they were controlled, carried along, driven and guided by the Holy Spirit. So we see, then, that it is the Holy Spirit himself who has given us the word.

Obviously, therefore, when the Holy Spirit works in us he

does so through his own word. He does his work of sanctification in us by leading us to contemplate the truth that he has
recorded in this word. So we become sanctified and are dealt
with by the Holy Spirit, not by contemplating beautiful
thoughts, not by some sort of science of the mind, cogitating on
the beautiful and the prophetic, turning our minds away from
that which is hurtful to the beautiful, and training our minds to
it – that is not the work of the Holy Spirit. Rather, the Holy
Spirit always directs us to the truth, the truth that he himself has
given, that he himself has inspired men to write. Therefore,
whatever you and I may feel, if it is not directly related to this
truth, it is not the work of the Holy Spirit.

There I think we see very clearly the difference between the
Christian message and that of any of the popular cults that are
in the world today. These cults do undoubtedly influence
people and make them feel much better. This is very good
psychology, because it is a good psychological rule always to
look on the bright side of things and to think beautiful thoughts
– it would be nonsense to deny that. But though you may be
doing that and may be feeling better physically, and better in
every respect as the result of cultivating beautiful thoughts, it
need have no connection whatsoever with the Christian faith
and the Christian message. Indeed, it may even be the greatest
hindrance to that message. The Christian message and the
Christian way of salvation is directly connected with this truth
from beginning to end. Beautiful thoughts may do you good,
but the question is: are those thoughts centred on the wonderful
works of God? Is your happiness based upon what God has
done, upon the activity of this mighty God, and the things that
are freely given us of God? The Spirit always directs to the
word.

But my second point is even more important: the Spirit not
only always directs us to the word, he always directs us, in particular, to what is, after all, the special message of this Word –
the Person of our blessed Lord and Saviour Jesus Christ. 'But I
thought,' says someone, 'that you were preaching exclusively
about the Holy Spirit, at this point.' But I cannot do that,

because our Lord himself told us that when the Holy Spirit came he would not speak of himself. This means not only that he will not speak from himself, but also that he will not speak about himself or about what he is going to do. Our Lord tell us, 'he shall testify of me' (Jn 15:26), and 'he shall glorify me' (Jn 16:14). The special work of the Holy Spirit is never to direct attention to himself, but always to direct it to the Lord Jesus Christ.

Peter, again, said: 'The God of our fathers raised up Jesus, whom ye slew and hanged on a tree. Him hath God exalted with his right hand to be a Prince, and a Saviour, for to give repentance to Israel, and forgiveness of sins. And we [the apostles] are his witnesses of these things; and so is also the Holy Ghost, whom God hath given to them that obey him' (Acts 5:30–32). 'We,' says Peter, in effect, 'were witnesses of the Lord Jesus Christ. We spent three years with him; we are telling you about him, what he did and said. We saw him nailed to a tree, and die upon the tree; we saw them take down his body and put it in a grave. We saw the stone rolled away, yes, and we were together in a room when he came into it, even though the doors were shut; and he appeared to us on other occasions too. We are witnesses of these things and so also is the Holy Spirit.' The Holy Spirit is a witness to these things, even as the apostles were. You will find that the author of the epistle to the Hebrews says exactly the same thing. He talks about the gospel which, he says, 'At the first began to be spoken by the Lord, and was confirmed unto us by them that heard him; God also bearing them witness both with signs and wonders, and with divers miracles, and gifts of the Holy Ghost' (Heb 2:3–4).

Indeed, the apostle John is most specific on this point, writing, in 1 John 4:2: 'Every spirit that confesseth that Jesus Christ is come in the flesh is of God.' This, therefore, is the vital test which we must always apply: the Holy Spirit always points to and glorifies the Lord Jesus Christ. Therefore when we come to test ourselves and ask ourselves, 'Have I received the Spirit, is the Spirit working in me?' the question I ask myself is not, 'What feelings do I have?' There are many agencies that will give me wonderful feelings, the cults, for instance, or poetry can give wonderful feelings, so can a sunset and so can drugs. Feelings are not the test. The Holy Spirit does give feelings, thank God, but the question I ask is this: 'If I have a feeling of joy and happiness, is it because of the Lord Jesus Christ, or is it not?' If I cannot directly relate my happiness, my joy, my peace, my all, to my blessed Lord, it is probably the spirit of anti-Christ and it has nothing to do with God at all. For the Holy Spirit always glorifies the Lord Jesus Christ.

The same applies to gifts. There are many agencies that can give men wonderful gifts, but unless these gifts are directly related to the Lord himself, they are not of God. I will go even further and say without any hesitation that you may have experiences of conquered sins and wonderful deliverances from things that have got you down for years, but I still assert solidly that it is not sanctification unless it is directly related to the Lord Jesus Christ. For I would remind you again that there are many cults that can deliver you from various sins. There are many things in this world that have enabled people to give up particular sins. You can read their stories, and you will find that the Lord Jesus Christ is not mentioned at all. So I assert that if the Lord Jesus Christ is not at the centre, if the glory is not given to him, it is not the work of the Holy Spirit, for the Holy Spirit always glorifies him. He always puts him in the centre, and brings us into relationship with him.

Thus, the Holy Spirit came in order to reveal Christ to us. His primary work is to make Christ real to us, to show us what Christ has done for us, to remind us of his teaching, to give us a longing and a love for Christ, to enable us to live as Christ lived, to conform us to his image – it is all centred on the Lord Jesus Christ. That is why I say with such emphasis that I must never isolate the doctrine of the Holy Spirit. Whatever I may think I have, whatever experience I think I may have, if I have the Holy Spirit, he will make me centre it all upon the Lord Jesus Christ, for he always leads to him. The other spirits do not, they say 'Glorify me.'

If you want to know whether you have the Holy Spirit and whether he is in you and dealing with you, that is the only safe and valid test. Feelings come and go, gifts come and go, you can become devout and careful in your life without him, but the hallmark of the work of the Holy Spirit is that he presents the Lord Jesus Christ to us, and brings us to an ever-increasing intimacy with him, and an enjoyment of his glorious presence. The Spirit sanctifies us by bringing us to the word, the word that brings us to a knowledge of him.

5

Different in Everything[1]

Submit yourselves to every ordinance of man for the Lord's sake: whether it be to the king, as supreme; or unto governors, as unto them that are sent by him for the punishment of evildoers, and for the praise of them that do well. For so is the will of God, that with well doing ye may put to silence the ignorance of foolish men: as free, and not using your liberty for a cloke of maliciousness, but as the servants of God. Honour all men. Love the brotherhood. Fear God. Honour the king (1 Peter 2:13-17).

So far, our studies in this seventeenth chapter of John have convinced us that the fundamental thing about the Christian is that he is one who is sanctified, sanctified by God; and to be sanctified means to be separated from the world and from sin and separated unto God. That is the scriptural teaching everywhere about the Christian, and we are reminded of that very forcibly in 1 Peter 2:13-17, and indeed, in the whole chapter, which we shall be looking at together. The Christian is a new creation: in the world but not of it; he is a man still, and yet he is not as he was. His fundamental postulate is, 'I live; yet not I, but Christ liveth in me' (Gal 2:20) – that is the essential meaning of sanctification – so that the Christian is different in every respect from the non-Christian. And there is nothing more

---

[1] This sermon was preached in 1953, on the Sunday before the Queen's coronation.

important, as I understand the New Testament teaching, and especially the teaching of the apostles, than that we should always be conscious of this, and that our entire lives may be governed by that realisation.

Now when I say that the Christian is one who is different in *every* respect, I use my words advisedly – '... if any man be in Christ, he is a new creation: old things are passed away; behold all things are become new' (2 Cor 5:17). And that word 'all' is as inclusive and as comprehensive as a word can be; everything is new and everything is different if we are truly Christian. And we all of us betray whether we are Christian or not, by every-thing we do and say, and by what we are. Our Lord taught on one occasion, you remember, that we shall all be judged by every idle word that we have uttered, and 'idle' means not pre-meditated, our casual words, our casual actions (see Matthew 12:36). The fact is that we are all along betraying what we are by our reaction to things, by our conduct and by our behaviour, and it is very interesting indeed to observe this. Our spirituality, ultimately, should be estimated and measured by the consis-tency of the whole of our life and living. There are people who, as it were, have to put on their Christianity for the time being, but if you see them in their casual moments, in their ordinary daily lives, you might perhaps not even suspect that they are Christians at all – they are living in compartments. But the more spiritual, the more sanctified we become, the more are we characterised by a wholeness and consistency, and it shows itself in all we do, and in our reaction to everything.

In the same way, and this has a particularly powerful emphasis in the New Testament, our thinking is governed by a new principle. Our whole outlook is new, we do not see things as we used to see them, nor do we see them as the natural man sees them. We were once governed by the world and its outlook, but that is no longer true of us. Notice how Peter puts that in verse 10: 'Which in time past were not a people, but are now the people of God: which had not obtained mercy, but now have obtained mercy.' In other words, as the result of regeneration, as the result of the operation of the Spirit of God upon them, and as a result of the fact that they are now partakers of the divine nature and have been born from above and of the Spirit, Christians must of necessity see things in an entirely new way. Their whole perspective is different, everything takes on a new colour. In particular, of course, we can put it like this: Christians are those whose outlook on all matters is to be controlled and governed entirely by the teaching of the Scriptures. They do not revert to the world in any respect at all. They must not merely say, 'I do not take the worldly view about certain practices,' the scriptural teaching is that they must not take the worldly view about *anything*. Not only do they not take the worldly view about things that are bad, they do not take the worldly view about things that are good either. Their outlook upon life is a totality, and it is entirely determined by the teaching of the Bible; they are men and women of one Book, and their whole outlook conforms to this.

Now this is clearly a very important principle, and it applies not only to the individual but also to the church and to the message and preaching of the church. These, too, are to be determined and controlled by nothing but the word of God. Our forefathers had to fight for this. As a result, today the state does not govern the preaching of the church and it must never be allowed to do so. There is no power on earth or among men which can be allowed to determine the message of the Christian church. The message of the preacher should be God-given and Spirit-inspired, and he must be controlled entirely and exclusively by the word as it comes to him and is brought to him by the Holy Spirit of God. We, therefore, are not controlled and governed by times and seasons or by circumstances. The tragedy of the Christian church has been that for so long she has indulged in what is called 'topical preaching', messages determined by the things that are happening around and about her, rather than the message which comes from God – the burden of the Lord; our preaching must always be out of the word, from the word, Spirit-inspired and Spirit-led.

So, then, we turn to the word, and the word speaks and takes hold of us, and we find that it teaches very plainly and clearly that our sanctification is something that applies to the whole of our lives and to every facet and aspect of our activities as human beings in this world. This is the glory of the Scriptures; no human relationship, no eventuality can possibly meet us, but that we find instruction concerning it somewhere in the word. And the word gives us very particular and definite instruction and teaching with regard to our relationship to the state, our relationship to the world in which we are bound to live and the country to which we are bound to belong; the word of God does not leave us without guidance.

This is something that many people seem never to have realised. They regard the Bible as if it had but the one theme of personal salvation: that is an utter travesty of the truth. The great primary and central theme is, of necessity, personal salvation, but the Bible does not stop at that. It gives teaching and instruction for this personal, saved life, as it is lived in this world, in its relationship, as we see in 1 Peter 2, with kings, with authorities and powers, with masters and servants – every conceivable relationship in life. It is an essential part of our sanctification to realise that we are to be governed by the word and its teaching in every relationship, and there is no exception whatsoever.

Therefore, I want to call your attention in particular, at this point, to the way in which our sanctification is shown, and is encouraged and developed, with respect to this whole matter of our relationship to the country to which we belong, the state under which we happen to be living. There are two main principles here. The first is that we must realise clearly that the church, the gospel, has only one message to the world and for the world. We must always start there. The Scriptures speak directly to individuals, not to nations or states; I cannot see that there is any message at all in the New Testament for nations as such. There is of course, in that respect, a difference between the Old Testament and the New; the church in the Old Testament was a particular nation, a particular state. But that is no longer the case, because, as Peter writes in this chapter, there is now a new nation: 'But ye are a chosen generation, a royal priesthood,

an holy nation' (1 Pet 2:9). The words in Exodus 19 that were
spoken to the children of Israel only are here spoken by the apostle Peter under divine inspiration and applied to this new nation,
the church. In Matthew 22:43 our Lord himself said that the
kingdom should be taken from the Jews and given to another
nation, and this other nation is clearly the Christian church,
which consists of men and women called out of every nation
under heaven. Consequently, we have this new situation, that
the New Testament does not address its remarks and its teaching to nations and to states, but primarily to individuals. It is a
personal message calling men and women out of different
nations into a new nation, this new kingdom in the Lord Jesus
Christ.

If that is so, then there are certain deductions which we must
draw quite inevitably, one of which is that there can be no scriptural authority for calling this nation, or any other country at the
present time, to an 'act of rededication'; such a thing seems to
me to be quite inconceivable and meaningless and indeed anti-
scriptural. As the New Testament speaks not to nations, but to
individuals, it has no 'call to rededication' to a nation as such,
because as I want to try to show you, that is something of which
the nation is incapable.

In the same way, therefore, I would argue that we cannot be
party to any call to people, 'whatever their religion', to pray
God's blessing upon our country. For, as I understand the New
Testament and its teaching, that again is a non-Christian statement. The church does not call upon all people 'whatever their
religion' to pray for God's blessing upon our country, and for
this good reason: that as Christians we say there is only one
faith. We do not recognise any other religion, indeed, we say
that all other religions are false: 'There is none other name under
heaven given among men, whereby we must be saved' (Acts
4:12), save that of the Lord Jesus Christ. So we send our missionaries to every country, whether Hindu, or Moslem or Con-
fucian, because we say and believe that those religions are not
true – there is only 'one mediator between God and men, the
man Christ Jesus' (1 Tim 2:5). We assert that these people are

worshipping God in a false manner and we send our missionaries to teach and train and enlighten them. We know that there is only one way to God in the Lord Jesus Christ, for, 'No man hath seen God at any time; the only begotten Son, which is in the bosom of the Father, he hath declared him' (Jn 1:18); and again, 'I am the way, the truth and the life; no man cometh unto the Father, but by me' (Jn 14:6) – so, as Christians, if we believe these things, we clearly and obviously cannot appeal to people of 'any religion whatsoever' to pray God's blessing upon us as a nation and as a people. It is tremendously important that our thinking should be governed by the Scriptures lest we contradict ourselves; lest, on the one hand, we send missionaries to convert people to the Christian faith, but then, at the same time, treat them as if they were on an equality with us in the matter of our approach to God.

Then we move on from that to the following proposition. The gospel of Jesus Christ, the Christian church, has but one message to the world, which is to warn men and women of the wrath to come, to proclaim to them that they are moving in the direction of the Day of Judgement, and to call upon them to realise that they have immortal souls for which they will have to answer in the presence of God. The church calls them, therefore, to repentance and to faith in the Lord Jesus Christ. Surely, as Christians we must take this position: if a man is not a Christian he is fundamentally wrong. He may be a good man, a moral man, he may be a good citizen in general. But we are not primarily interested in him as such, we are interested in him as a soul, and we know that no man can truly be the citizen he should be until he is a Christian; he is failing at some point or other. The message is that we become good and noble and true citizens to the extent that we are loyal and obedient servants to our Lord and Saviour Jesus Christ. Men and women who are not Christians in this nation today cannot rededicate themselves to God. They must repent, they must come before God on bended knee and recognise that they have sinned against him and that they have forgotten him. They must be born again. I cannot call them to any act of rededication or reconsecration because they must go down before they can rise; they must repent before they can be received; they must believe on the Lord Jesus Christ as their only Saviour, Redeemer and Lord. The Christian message does not vary because of circumstances; and that is the unchanging message of the Christian church to the world and to men and women in this nation who are not Christians.

But that is only the beginning. Having said that the church has only one message for the world, I now go on to ask, what, then, is the relationship of the Christian to the state and to these other things? We have seen the position of the non-Christian, but what is that of the Christian? And here it seems to me that the teaching of this verse in 1 Peter, as indeed the teaching of the entire Scriptures, can be summarised under a number of very definite propositions. The first is that we must start with our basic position as Christians. Peter says, 'Dearly beloved, I beseech you as strangers and pilgrims ...' (1 Pet 2:11) – that is the basic position. Our relationship to the world is determined and governed by that definition. As Christians we are but strangers and pilgrims, travellers and sojourners in this world of time.

Or again, the apostle Paul puts it still more specifically in Philippians 3:20 where he says, 'Our conversation [our citizenship] is in heaven,' or, if you prefer it, 'we are a colony of heaven'. That is our fatherland, the state to which we belong: our citizenship is in heaven. And you notice how the apostle rejoices in the fact that he, who was once such a zealous, narrow-minded Jew, can now say: 'there is neither Jew nor Greek' (Gal 3:28), and, indeed, still more specifically, 'where there is neither Greek nor Jew, circumcision nor uncircumcision, Barbarian, Scythian, bond nor free: but Christ is all and in all' (Col 3:11). Then in Ephesians 2 he rejoices in the fact that the middle wall of partition which hitherto had divided the Jews from the Gentiles has been broken down. It was once there in the Temple itself but it has now been demolished.

How, then, do we interpret these statements (and they are but a selection from a number of similar statements which I might have put to you)? It seems to me that we must put it like this:

as Christians, our first and highest loyalty must always, inevitably, be to God and his Christ; that must come even before our loyalty to country and to king or queen. Our loyalty to God and Christ comes before our loyalty to any nationality; we are primarily the people of God, we are his special possession. He has taken hold of us and brought us out of these various natural relationships into this special, personal relationship to himself. Therefore in all my thinking I must start with that – that is the thing which is to control me and govern me, and I must never think or do anything which violates that preliminary, fundamental postulate.

Then, of course, that position works itself out in this way. We have been delivered – as G K Chesterton put it – 'that we might be delivered from pride and from blind prejudice'. I do not want to elaborate all this now, because I am anxious to give you a number of headings. But I think we must all know that the great cause of warfare and turmoil, and difficult and troublesome times, is pride, whether between individuals or between nations. Indeed, there can be little doubt but that the most prolific cause of war, in both the ancient and the modern world is a narrow nationalism. The tragedy is, of course, that we all recognise that in others, but are not always so ready to see it in ourselves. I am sure that in general all of us are prepared to denounce narrow nationalism, but how difficult it is to 'see ourselves as others see us'. Yet the New Testament, bringing us fundamentally into our relationship to God, makes it impossible for any Christian to say 'my country right or wrong'. Christians cannot say that because to do so would be to deny their own faith. They have been delivered from every natural pride, indeed, they regard all such things as their greatest enemy, the biggest obstacle to their true growth in grace, and to their sanctification. They are anxious, therefore, that they may be delivered from hatred, from despising others, and from glorying in the flesh in any shape or form – they see that all these things are antagonistic to the Spirit of Christ and of God.

Christians are those who see themselves as sinners. Our Lord starts off the Sermon on the Mount by saying, 'Blessed are the poor in spirit' (Matt 5:3) – and those who are poor in spirit are people who do not take any pride in themselves, in what they are or what they have done. They are not always beating the big drum about their own achievements and their greatness and superiority to others – they are the very antithesis of that. Christians see themselves as sinners with nothing to boast of, they know that what they need above everything else is the new nature, the rebirth; they thank God for it, and they give their primary, fundamental loyalty to God. And because they rejoice above everything else in the fact that they are now citizens of the heavenly kingdom, they have been emancipated from that tendency to pride, self-satisfaction and conceit, from hatred and from despising of others. They are totally unlike the Pharisee in our Lord's story, for the Pharisee thanked God that he was not like other people, because he had done this and that, while the other man had done nothing. And what Christians think about themselves as individuals, applies also to the way they regard their nation. Their thinking is consistent and it is worked out in the whole of life and in every relationship.

Then I go one step further. Because Christians glory in the Lord, because this is their fundamental loyalty, they feel the bond of unity, fellowship and brotherhood with those who belong to Christ in any nation whatsoever. They feel this deeply and in a more real sense than they feel any natural ties or bonds. Now this is strong doctrine, but our Lord put it like this: 'He that loveth father or mother more than me is not worthy of me: and he that loveth son or daughter more than me is not worthy of me' (Matt 10:37). Indeed, in one Gospel it says that we must *hate* father and mother for his sake – that is how our Lord puts it about the individual. We are to feel a relationship to him and a bond to him closer and dearer and more intimate and valuable than even the dearest earthly tie. If that, then, is to be true of us with regard to our closest and our dearest, how much more is it to be true of us in our relationship to those who are bound to us by general ties of nationality and country? Christians, therefore – and this is a test of the Christian – should feel more closely bound to a Christian from any country under the sun than they do to anyone who is not a Christian in their own country. Their loyalty to Christ comes before loyalty to country; their relationship to Christ and to all who are in Christ is bigger and more vital than the other relationship which belongs only to nature and to the flesh. These are some of the implications of this doctrine, and you see why I emphasised at the beginning that a Christian is a man whose outlook is governed everywhere by the teaching of Scripture.

'But,' someone may say, 'what about the apostle Paul in Romans 9, 10 and 11? Does he not there glory as a Jew, and does he not seem to put nationality into the first position?' The answer is, of course, that when the Apostle writes as he does about the Jews, he is referring to them as God's own people, not as Jews qua Jews, and not in any nationalistic sense. He writes as he does about them because they were God's chosen people, who were meant to be witnesses of God and of the coming Messiah, but who had failed to recognise him. Thus Paul's interest in them is a spiritual interest and not a mere national or natural one.

All these things show that our fundamental position, our basic loyalty, is to God and to the Lord Jesus Christ. But let me add that this does not mean that all these other relationships are abolished. This is a most important point – the balance of Scripture is most wonderful. Why did the apostle Peter write these words in the verses we are considering? Why do you think the apostle Paul does the same thing? There can be no doubt as to the answer. The early Christians, listening to the high doctrine which I have been expounding, were led into error by the devil, and were saying that because we are Christians we have nothing to do with these lands and nations to which we belong. Indeed, some of them, who were slaves, were saying that because they had become Christians they had no loyalty any longer to their masters, but could do as they pleased.

'Certainly not!' says the Scripture; that is an entirely false deduction. We are not to assume that all these other relationships have been abrogated, for they have not. We teach, on the basis of Scripture, that all the fundamental ordinances of God still stand. In other words, it is God who has divided the nations and placed their boundaries and brought them into being. It is he who has appointed legislators and decreed that there should be kings and governments and authorities and powers – these are all ordained of God. It is the scriptural teaching that there shall be magistrates. Even though the magistrates may not be Christians, while I am a Christian, I must nevertheless obey them, and the laws of the land, because Scripture tells me to do so. We are to conform to all these things. Peter even tells these servants to be subject to their masters, not only to the good and gentle but also to the 'froward' or harsh (2:18).

Some of the first Christians were obviously arguing about these things. Some had been brought up under paganism. They were married people, but now that they had become Christians, some of the married men tended to leave their wives because they were unconverted. But the teaching of Scripture is that a man is not bound to leave his wife because he is a Christian and she is not. In other words, these natural human relationships are not abolished, instead, the teaching is, clearly, that we must look upon them in a new way. We do not become anarchists because we are Christians. We do not say that we refuse to recognise any law or authority or power at all – that is as wrong as to remain in the other natural position, which we have already criticised and dealt with. The apostle Paul uses a phrase which seems to me to sum up the true Christian position perfectly – we are to 'use this world as not abusing it' (1 Cor 7:31). In other words, all our conduct is to be controlled by this new point of view, and if we are only governed by this, we shall never go astray.

Take, then, our relationship to the Queen and to the government and to the various authorities in this country, how are we to carry it out? Well, this is how Scripture puts it – 'Submit yourselves to every ordinance of man *for the Lord's sake*: whether it be to the king, as supreme; or unto governors, as unto them that are sent by him for the punishment of evildoers, and for the praise of them that do well' (1 Pet 2:13–14). It is, in other words, for the Lord's sake that we do these things; we do not do it simply because it is our country or our Queen or our government. Everything we do, we do for the Lord's sake, and you will find the same teaching with respect to our duties to masters and servants and so on. Our reason for submitting ourselves to human ordinances is entirely different from that of the non-Christian; he does it with his worldly, carnal, fleshly motive, whereas we do everything for the Lord's sake. We obey the Queen, we submit to the government, in order that we may tell forth his praise who has called us out of darkness into his most marvellous light. We do all these things as an opportunity of showing what God has done to us and for us in the Lord Jesus Christ. This is something that governs us everywhere.

But I must go on to add that if we should ever reach a point at which any authority that is above us should ask us to disobey God, then we must refuse, because our primary and fundamental loyalty is to God and not to any human authority. Let me quote the words of the apostle Peter in Acts 4:19: 'Whether it be right in the sight of God to hearken unto you more than unto God, judge ye ...' The authorities were trying to prohibit him and his fellow apostles from preaching the Lord Jesus Christ and that is his reply. In Acts 5:29 he puts it like this: 'We ought to obey God rather than men.' And our forefathers have had occasion in times past to utter the same words. Thank God, we have no occasion to utter them in our country at this present time, but our gospel is for all times and should a time ever come in our country when we have to face the choice of obeying God or obeying the most august human authority, we, as Christian people, must always obey God, whatever the cost. So let us at this moment give honour to those men and women in other lands and countries who are doing this very thing at this very hour. Let us not forget the doctrine. We live in this way because of our fundamental postulate that now we look at nothing as the world looks at it. Rather, we look at everything through spiritual eyes, because we are controlled by the fact that our ultimate loyalty is to God and to the Lord Jesus Christ.

Therefore, finally, we can put it like this: we obey all these ordinances of man for the Lord's sake. Let us remember that we do everything in the fear of the Lord. The Christian should never do anything in a worldly spirit. He should not honour the Queen in a worldly spirit; he should not do anything as the world does it, for he does everything in the fear of God, as one in whom the Holy Spirit dwells. His conception of citizenship and of loyalty is determined not by the mind and outlook and spirit of the world, but by the Spirit that is of God.

So the Christian, you see, is a unique person. He is not merely a new man, but also a new creation. He both thinks in a different way, and does everything in a different way. May God grant that in all we think, and in all we do, we may always make it evident that we are these 'peculiar', special, spiritual people. 'Dearly beloved, I beseech you as strangers and pilgrims' – it is we alone who realise that that is the truth. The world never stops to think about that, but we know that we are sojourners and pilgrims in this world. So, 'abstain from fleshly lusts' – in every form – 'which war against the soul; having your conversation honest among the Gentiles: that, whereas they speak against you as evildoers, they may by your good works, which they shall behold, glorify God in the day of visitation' (vv. 11-12). The Christian is always different and he is different in everything.

6

The Yearning of the Holy Spirit

Sanctify them through thy truth: thy word is truth (John 17:17).

As we continue with our study of the work of the Holy Spirit in our sanctification, let me remind you that we have seen clearly that we must never isolate this doctrine and regard it as something separate and distinct. The Holy Spirit has been sent and is among us to glorify the Lord Jesus Christ, and we must never think of sanctification and holiness apart from him. We saw, secondly, how the Holy Spirit guided the 'holy men of God' as they wrote the Scriptures, and kept them from error; and then we considered together how he works in us through the word.

Let us proceed, then, from that point, but let me remind you that we are not here considering the whole doctrine of the Holy Spirit. We know something of the work of the Spirit in creation, and in many other respects, but we are now concerned in particular with the work of the Holy Spirit in sanctification, and are confining our attention to that.

So we come once more to the question of how the Holy Spirit carries out this work in us. I need scarcely remind you that it is a subject which has often been misunderstood and has often led to disagreement. It has provoked much discussion and has produced many errors and heresies in the Christian church, and still tends to do so. It is, indeed, as has often been pointed out, a very remarkable thing that this truth, which of all others was meant to demonstrate unity, has perhaps caused more division than any other particular aspect of the truth. It was the Holy Spirit who produced that great and amazing unity on the Day of Pentecost. On that day, men of different nations were all made one by this power, and yet, since then, because of the misunderstanding of the doctrine, it has often led not only to disagreement, but even to schism. We must therefore approach it with caution, and be very careful to allow the Scriptures to speak to us.

I would suggest to you that an important principle stands out very clearly in scriptural teaching with regard to this subject. This is that the Holy Spirit dwells within all Christians. Now this is a most important point. There are people who would have you believe that you can be a Christian without receiving the Holy Spirit. But that is thoroughly unscriptural. I would affirm once more that it is impossible for us to be Christians at all without having the Holy Spirit in us. Let me give you some of the Scriptures which assert this. In 1 Corinthians 12:3 we read, 'No man can say that Jesus is the Lord, but by the Holy Ghost.' No man can *really* say; it does not just mean that you say it with your lips, because obviously a blasphemer and unbeliever could utter these words – but if when he says it a man really means it, then that man can say 'Jesus is Lord' only by the Holy Spirit. But the Apostle is still more explicit in Romans 8:9: 'If any man have not the Spirit of Christ, he is none of his.' Now there we have a categorical statement to the effect that if a man does not have the Holy Spirit of Christ within him, he is not a Christian at all, and does not belong to Christ. So it is surely the height of folly, and a complete error, to suggest that one can be a Christian and then later receive the Holy Spirit – we cannot be Christians at all apart from the Holy Spirit, and his work in us and upon us.

But let me give you some more passages, for this is a vital subject. In 1 Corinthians 12:13 the Apostle teaches, 'For by one Spirit are we all baptised into one body.' Christians are members of the body of Christ; 'Ye,' he says in 1 Corinthians 12:27, addressing the church, addressing Christians, 'Ye are the body of Christ, and members in particular.' Thus, to be a Christian means to be a part of the body of Christ, and how does this happen to us? The answer is: 'By one Spirit are we all baptised into one body.' In other words, the point we are emphasising is that by definition, we cannot be Christian at all except the Holy Spirit should thus have put us into this one body of Christ.

Then again, in 1 Corinthians 6:19 the Apostle Paul says: 'What? know ye not that your body is the temple of the Holy Ghost which is in you, which ye have of God, and ye are not your own?' He is writing there to the members of the church at Corinth, not to some of them, but to all of them, and he is writing about a most unpleasant and unsavoury subject. He is particularly warning them against the sin of fornication, of which some of them had been guilty, and his argument is: This is impossible, you must not do this. Do you not know that your body is the temple of the Holy Spirit, and for this reason you cannot be joined in that way to a harlot? He reminds these members of the church at Corinth, many of whom were guilty of such extraordinary sins and weaknesses, that even their bodies are the temples of the Holy Spirit which God has given them and that, therefore, the Holy Spirit is in them. Our Lord had promised this particularly. He had promised his disciples that if they believed in him, he would give them the Holy Spirit.

But let me give you one more quotation, which again is very striking, and this time it is found in James 4:5. In the Authorised Version it reads like this: 'The Spirit that dwelleth in us lusteth to envy', but I think it is generally agreed that that is not the best translation at that point. It ought to be put like this: 'The Spirit which he made to dwell in us yearneth over us even unto jealous envy.' The point I am emphasising at this moment is 'the Spirit that he made to dwell in us' – again, a statement that the Holy Spirit is resident in all Christian people.

I could give you other quotations, but let those be sufficient. The point I am anxious to establish, and you will appreciate what an important one it is, is that we must lay down the basic position that it is impossible to be a Christian at all unless the Holy Spirit is in us; for to be a Christian means that the Holy Spirit has taken up his abode in us. Or take the way John puts it. He says in chapter 2:17 of his first epistle that all Christians have received the anointing of the Holy Spirit. John's epistle is to all Christians, and their understanding is dependent upon the fact that they have received the anointing, they have received this gift which the Lord Jesus Christ promised that he himself would give to all who believe in him.

So, then, if that proposition is true, we can proceed to ask our vital question: how does the Holy Spirit do this work of sanctification within us? Now here we find two remarkable, scriptural, statements. I have already quoted one of them, James 4:5, and I want to put this very plainly. The Authorised Version, you remember, says, 'The Spirit that dwelleth in us lusteth to envy,' but I have suggested that a better translation is, 'The Spirit which he made to dwell in us yearneth over us even unto a jealous envy.' Then I want to take with that verse a statement made in Galatians 5:17 where we read that 'the flesh lusteth against the Spirit, and the Spirit against the flesh.'

Now there, it seems to me, is the basic position with regard to the work of the Holy Spirit in our sanctification. We are told that the Holy Spirit, who has been given to us by the Lord Jesus Christ, has been given in order that he may produce our sanctification. It is thus that God sanctifies us. In the first place, we are told that the Holy Spirit within us is yearning for our sanctification with a jealous envy. Look at it like this. The Holy Spirit comes into us, but by nature, and as a result of sin and the Fall, we are fleshly, we are all creatures of lust, and not only lust of the flesh but also of the mind. That is the teaching of the apostle Paul in Ephesians 2:3; we were all, he says, subject to these lusts and we all know this very well from experience. We are governed by passions; there are lusts and there are desires within us, and of course the world and the flesh and the devil play an equal part. There are these promptings, these desires, these evil powers within us striving for mastery over us.

Then into all that comes the Holy Spirit of God, and the Holy Spirit is a Person. He is not a mere power, nor just an influence, but a Person. Our Lord, you remember, told the disciples just as he was leaving them, 'Let not your heart be troubled ...' I am going to leave you but, 'I will pray the Father, and he shall give you another Comforter' (Jn 14:1, 16), another Person and he will do certain things for you and to you.

So these two statements tell us that as the flesh is there lusting within us and drawing us away from God, and into sin and evil, so the Holy Spirit is yearning for us, desiring the mastery over us, desiring to control us, desiring us for God and for Christ. He yearns over us, he desires us – the word that is really used is 'lusteth' – even to a jealous envy. In other words, the Spirit of God, and of Christ, and the Holy Spirit, the three Persons in the blessed Holy Trinity, desire us. The Holy Spirit sees these evil influences in us and he hates them, and is yearning to deliver us from them and to set us on the other side. The Holy Spirit is opposed to everything that represents the world and the flesh and the devil. He is against everything in us that is opposed to God, and his work within us is to deliver us from these evil things and to emancipate us from them in order to make us what God intends us to be, and to accomplish what the Lord Jesus Christ has died for.

There, then, is the great truth, and to me it is one of the most comforting, consoling and wonderful truths that a Christian can ever discover; that as a Christian I no longer just live to myself, I have the Holy Spirit dwelling within me, lusting, striving, yearning, that there is this blessed conflict. Indeed, unless we know something about this conflict we obviously are not Christians at all, for it is there in every Christian. Once we were only the flesh, now we are spirit and flesh and these two are opposed to one another. There is the flesh dragging us, drawing us down, and the Spirit drawing us up. There is a fight going on within, because the Holy Spirit has come into us to reside within us, and God does this work of sanctification within us, through this energy and activity, through this longing of the Spirit within us.

So now, if that is the great general principle of the Holy Spirit's work in us, how does he do it in particular? We can divide his method up very simply. The first thing he does is to call our attention to the truth, all of the truth which we have been considering, the amazing truth about the being and the character and the nature of God, and, too, the truth about sin. We can never know the truth about God, and about sin, until we find it in this word of God. It is the Spirit who gave the word and it is he who leads us to it, to this great word about the Lord Jesus Christ, his Person and his work – it is the Spirit that leads us to that. By nature I am not interested in those things. By nature I like to read the newspaper, all the detailed reports of the Law Courts, and about what the world is doing with all its gaiety and pleasure. I do not want to read this word, but the Spirit leads me to it. His work is to glorify Christ, to reveal him and all the other great and rich doctrines that we have been studying – it is the Spirit who calls my attention to the word, and who goes on drawing my attention to it for every detail of my life.

It is the Spirit, also, who shows me my position as a Christian: this extraordinary doctrine of my being placed in Christ, of my relationship to Christ as a branch in the vine, I in Christ and Christ in me. No man could think of that or discover it, and no man has ever done so. It is the Spirit who leads on to these things, and it is extraordinary, as we examine our experience, to see how he does that. Has this not often surprised you? Here we are, we have had an open Bible before us all our lives, with all these rich truths and doctrines; and yet must we not all admit, as we look back across our lives to having this kind of experience. One day we read a passage, and suddenly we were led to see some great truth, but then we seemed to stop there, we did not do anything about it. Years passed by, and then one day that truth dawned upon us again and we were called to see it and to act upon it. It is always the work of the Spirit: he presents the truth to us. Sometimes we brush it aside and show that we are not interested in it, but he keeps on bringing it back – not only directly by the word but by a book, maybe, that someone brings to our notice. It is all the work of the Spirit. He puts the truth before us, he presents it and shows us these great possibilities that are there for us.

Furthermore, we must not stay even with that. The Holy Spirit not only puts the truth before us and leads us to it, it is he alone who enables us to understand the truth. Now that is the great theme of 1 Corinthians 2, a vital passage in this connection. The Apostle writes there that 'The natural man receiveth not the things of the Spirit of God: for they are foolishness unto him: neither can he know them, because they are spiritually discerned' (1 Cor 2:14). He comes to us: 'We have received, not the spirit that is of the world, but the spirit which is of God' – why? – 'that we might know the things that are freely given to us of God' (v. 12), and we will never know these things apart from the anointing of the Holy Spirit. You can talk to the natural man at his highest and his best, you can talk to the world's greatest intellect and greatest philosopher, you can ask him to read the New Testament, and as a natural man he will know nothing about it. He will understand nothing at all about this amazing doctrine of what is possible to the Christian, for he cannot do so until he receives the Holy Spirit.

Then you may go to him and tell him about this wonderful truth – about the Christian being in Christ and Christ in the Christian – but to him it will be idle nonsense, mere rubbish, a fairy tale. He cannot receive it because he has not the gift of the Holy Spirit. We can only know these things that are given to us of God, and by God, as we have the Holy Spirit within us; these things are foolishness to the natural man, because his way of life consists only of amassing knowledge of truth and philosophy and then proceeding to apply it. That may be his idea, but it is not that of Scripture. The scriptural idea is to be baptised into Christ like the branch in the vine, and the love of Christ comes into us and fills us and does these wonderful things in us and through us. To the natural man that is foolishness, but we have the mind of Christ.

So we see that the Holy Spirit works in two ways. He leads me to the word, and then he does something to me which enables me to receive it. Thus it is that he goes on working within us, yearning with this jealous envy that we may be sanctified, and as I am led by him, I begin to understand this truth and to realise it. We see in Ephesians 3 that the apostle Paul was praying for the Ephesians that they might be 'filled with all the fulness of God' (v. 19), and as I realise that I am meant to be filled in that way, I begin to desire this and to hunger and thirst after it – but I would never have done so if the Holy Spirit had not been working within me. He leads me to the truth and then I desire it, and begin to long for it. Then I seek for it, and I hunger and thirst after righteousness. That is the method of the Spirit, and that is something of his procedure.

Let me remind you again of those well-known words in Philippians 2:12-13. The apostle Paul says, you remember, 'Work out your own salvation with fear and trembling. For it is God which worketh in you both to will and to do of his good pleasure.' That is a great statement. Let me give it to you again in a still better translation: God is one who through his Spirit is constantly supplying you with the impulse, giving you both the power to resolve, and the will and the strength to perform, from his good pleasure. He does it all. We must work it out with 'fear and trembling'; we do not remain passive but we work only because he is working in us the desire to work it out, and he gives us the power to do so.

And, finally, I would like to put it in this way – have you noticed the remarkable prayer of the Apostle in Ephesians 3, beginning at verse 14? Read it once more: 'For this ... cause I bow my knees unto the Father of our Lord Jesus Christ, of whom the whole family in heaven and earth is named, that he would grant you, according to the riches of his glory, to be strengthened with might by his Spirit in the inner man; that Christ may dwell in your hearts by faith; that ye, being rooted and grounded in love, may be able to comprehend with all saints what is the breadth, and length, and depth, and height; and to know the love of Christ which passeth knowledge, that ye might be filled with all the fulness of God.'

What does that mean? Let me put it simply like this. The real need, of course, of every Christian is that Christ may dwell in our hearts by faith; that is the extraordinary thing which he again promises. He has said to the disciples: It is good for you that I go away, but if I go away I will send him unto you.

This is why the Comforter comes. The astounding thing that

the Scripture offers me is that the Lord Jesus Christ should come and dwell in me here on earth. How can he do this? Knowing myself as I am, and what I am, as the result of sin and the Fall, I say it is impossible, and it is impossible apart from the work of the Holy Spirit, who strengthens me with his own power in the inner man, in order that Christ may dwell in my heart by faith. What a wonderful picture this is! The work of the Holy Spirit in men is to prepare a home for the Lord Jesus Christ. He is the servant who is sent along to prepare the palace for the King, to put it in order, to make everything fit and meet, to get rid of all that is unworthy. That is his purpose. The supreme height of sanctification and of holiness is that Christ dwells in us, living his life in us and through us. 'I live; yet not I, but Christ liveth in me' (Gal 2:20) – that is the height of Christian achievement.

And this is how it becomes possible. We need to be strengthened by might, by the Holy Spirit, in the inner man, in order that Christ may dwell in our hearts by faith, so that Christ may take up his abode with us as a permanent guest – not come and go, but abide – settle down. Here in Ephesians 3:17 the Apostle is repeating Jesus' own word, and it is the Holy Spirit that makes that possible.

So we end as we began, by pointing out that all this must be thought of in terms of Persons. We must not think of our sanctification in terms of gifts or experience or anything like that. It is really being made fit and ready to receive the Lord Jesus Christ as the permanent guest in our hearts and in our inner man; and it is the Holy Spirit who does that work. He covets us for Christ, he yearns over us, and longs for us, 'he yearneth over us even unto jealous envy' that we may be Christ's and not the world's. And what he desires above everything else is that he may so deal with us and so work in us that we shall be ready to receive this heavenly guest himself, and he does that in the ways that I have been describing to you. He leads us to the truth, he enables us to receive it, giving us a longing and a hunger for it. He also gives us the power to do that. He undertakes for us and so he prepares us to receive the Lord Jesus Christ. That, then, is the work of the Holy Spirit, that is what he is yearning for and longing for us. Therefore, surely it comes to this: our greatest concern should be to conform to that and to allow the Spirit to do all his work in us.

7

Be Filled with the Spirit

Sanctify them through thy truth: thy word is truth (John 17:17).

In our continuing study of the work of the Holy Spirit in our sanctification I should like us at this point particularly to consider Ephesians 5:18. We finished our last study by emphasising the supreme importance of allowing the Holy Spirit to have his way with us, and we saw that the Scriptures are constantly exhorting us to do that. What we have in this particular verse is a very strong and graphic instance of that very teaching: 'Be not drunk with wine, wherein is excess; but be filled with the Spirit.' Now there are some preliminary remarks which we must make before we come to a detailed examination of this verse, and the first is to draw your attention to the setting. Here is a great statement which comes in that part of the epistle which is devoted to practicalities. The Apostle has dealt with the doctrine, and has now come to its application. He is dealing with details of conduct and behaviour and it is in the midst of such details that he introduces this sentence. In other words, he introduces this idea of being filled with the Spirit, not as some great doctrine standing apart on its own, but when he is dealing with ordinary life and living. Again, it rather suggests, does it not, that we must be very careful not to isolate this doctrine and put it in a compartment on its own. It is as we are living our ordinary lives that we realise this doctrine, this truth.

We notice also here the scriptural way of dealing with sins.

This verse comes in the midst of exhortations about what to drink and what not to drink, what to speak about, what is to interest and amuse us; exhortations about the duties of husbands towards their wives and wives towards their husbands – that is the context. Therefore we deduce that the scriptural way of dealing with all these problems is not so much to concentrate on the problems themselves, as to approach the whole of life in this positive way. We have been at pains to point out many times in the course of these studies on the question of sanctification that, surely, in the light of the Scriptures, any teaching must be wrong which concentrates primarily upon sins. Any holiness teaching or any doctrine of sanctification which begins by saying, 'Now about getting rid of that particular sin of yours,' is in itself starting in the wrong way. The scriptural method is positive; the way to deal with these things is to be filled with the Spirit.

There are many analogies which make it clear what I mean by that. For instance, there are two ways of facing the problem of physical disease or lack of health. You can deal with the infection, or whatever it is, directly, but the still better way, and the way which is increasingly used, is to concentrate on the positive concept of health. For far too long even medical science has been thinking in terms of diseases, but the better idea is to think in terms of health. Public health is rightly receiving more attention than it has ever done, for we should all be interested in being well, rather than in avoiding diseases. Now that is exactly what the Scripture does, because if you are, as Scripture enjoins, filled with the Spirit, then you will not be able to do these things, nor will you want to. The scriptural way of dealing with them is to clarify our thinking about these various sins, and it says: Can you not see that those things are incompatible with this great truth? The Apostle does exactly the same thing in his letter to the Galatians when he says, 'Walk in the Spirit, and ye shall not fulfil the lusts of the flesh' (Gal 5:16). If you want to avoid the pestilences and diseases that arise out of the swamps down in the valleys, the best thing to do is to walk to the top of the mountain. That is the way to look at it – the positive approach – being filled with the Spirit.

What, therefore, in detail and in practice, is the meaning of this exhortation, 'Be filled with the Spirit'? Very fortunately for us, the Apostle leads us into an understanding of his own exhortation by giving us an illustration: 'Be not drunk with wine wherein is excess, but be filled with the Spirit.' If we want to know what it means to be filled with the Spirit, let us make use of his own analogy. Here we would observe that this is not the only time that this analogy is used of the Spirit. On the Day of Pentecost, when the Holy Spirit descended upon the believers, the people in Jerusalem looked at them and said, 'These men are full of new wine' (Acts 2:13). The disciples behaved in a strange and unusual manner and the people jumped to the conclusion that they were drunk. But it was an explanation that was immediately dismissed by Peter. 'These,' he said, 'are not drunken, as ye suppose,' and then he went on to explain what had happened.

There is even, I think, the same suggestion in Luke 1:15 where the angel spoke to Zacharias about John the Baptist. There is at any rate an implied contrast between wine and strong drink on the one hand, and the Holy Spirit on the other, when Zacharias is told that his child who is to be born shall not partake of wine and strong drink, but shall be filled with the Holy Spirit. Thus it is obviously a helpful comparison.

What, then, does this suggest to us? Well, to be drunk with wine means that we are under its influence or control. To be drunk with wine means that our faculties, our mind, our feelings, our wills and our actions are all under another influence. This thing that the man has been drinking is now, as it were, controlling him; at least, that is the way in which we normally think of it. That is the illustration that Scripture itself uses in order to help us understand what it means to be filled with the Spirit.

But let me give you some other analogies which will suggest the same thing. For instance, we often speak about being 'full of life'. Or we say of certain people that at the moment they are really full of something. Someone maybe is proposing to take a holiday in the summer in some foreign land, and we say he is absolutely full of the idea. We mean by this that he is obviously possessed by it; every time you meet him he talks about it – he is full of it. Or we talk, in the same way, of being full of ideas, full of interests or even full of a person; the idea is that we are controlled by this interest or by this person, or whatever it may happen to be; we are full of it, it is the thing that absorbs and controls us.

Now the words that were used by the Apostle really do convey all that. The exact definition of the words would be something like this: anything that wholly takes possession of the mind, is said to 'fill the mind'; or, to put it another way: to be filled with anything means that it takes possession of us. That is what the Apostle tells us should be our relationship to the Holy Spirit. To be filled with the Spirit means to be controlled by him in that sense: we are filled with him and he controls our thoughts and minds, our emotions, our feelings, our desires, our words, our actions, our everything; it follows of necessity.

As you read the Scriptures and the examples and illustrations which it gives of this very thing, you see that that is exactly what is implied. We are told, for instance, of our Lord himself after his baptism, and after the Holy Spirit had descended upon him, that he, 'being full of the Holy Ghost returned from Jordan, and was led by the Spirit into the wilderness, being forty days tempted of the devil' (Lk 4:1-2). He returned from the Jordan filled with the Spirit, controlled and dominated by the Spirit for the work that lay ahead of him. There are, of course, many other examples of this. Take, for instance, what we are told of Stephen: we read that he was full of faith and of the Holy Spirit. We are told the same thing about Barnabas, that he was a good man and full of the Holy Spirit and of faith. There are also instances of Peter and Paul and other apostles, where we are told that 'filled with the Spirit' they did certain things.

The whole idea must be thought of in that way, and perhaps it is important that one should put it negatively at this point. Far too often, it seems to me, we tend to think of being filled with the Spirit in mechanical terms. The idea seems to be conjured up in our minds of an empty vessel and of something being poured into it. I think if you examine yourself and your thoughts, you will find that instinctively you tend to think of being filled with the Spirit in that way. We regard the Spirit as a kind of power that is poured into us; we are some kind of empty vessel and when we become empty, this Spirit, this power, this influence is poured into us until we are full. But clearly that must be wrong, because the Holy Spirit is not an influence, nor a power. We must not think of him in terms of electricity or of steam, for the Holy Spirit is a Person; he is described everywhere in the Scriptures in a personal manner. So when we think of being filled with the Spirit what we really mean is that the blessed Person of the Holy Spirit is controlling us, dominating and influencing us. That is why in my analogy I talked about being full of a certain person. We see that in everyday psychology. When a man becomes interested in some special person he is absolutely full of that person. It does not mean that the person is poured into him, but it does mean that the person is controlling his thoughts, his desires, and his activities, dominating the whole of his life and especially his thoughts. He is thus under the influence of and is being mastered by that person. I think you will find it is a very great advantage to have that conception clear in your mind, because most of the excesses and errors into which people have fallen with regard to this doctrine of being filled with the Spirit are almost invariably due to the fact that they think of the Spirit as some force or power that can be injected or transfused into us, instead of thinking of him in terms of this relationship to the Person who has been given to us and who dwells with us. This will become clearer as we proceed.

Let me, therefore, put a second proposition. What exactly are the results of this filling of the Spirit? For as we look at that, we shall find it will clarify our ideas. How do we know whether we are really filled with the Spirit or not? Once more, we can do nothing better than follow the examples which are provided for us in the text: 'Be not drunk with wine, wherein is excess; but be filled with the Spirit.' We are clearly confronted here by a similarity and contrast and we must pay careful attention to both. There is, as we have seen, something comparable between the influence of wine and strong drink upon a person and the effect of being filled with the Spirit. The analogy would never have been used, it would never have entered the mind of the crowd on the Day of Pentecost at Jerusalem, unless that were so. There are certain respects in which the similarity is very striking.

So that leads us to ask the question: what is the effect of wine or strong drink upon a person? Here again I must say something for the sake of accuracy and carefulness. When the Scriptures use an analogy and an illustration like this, they are obviously not speaking in a strict scientific sense. Rather, they are using the description in the way in which these things are commonly regarded. I emphasise all this because unless I safeguard myself at this point it could be said that my view of the effect of alcohol upon the body is not scientific.

But having said that by way of a preface, my first observation is that the effect of alcohol upon a man is to stimulate him. Now I am well aware of the fact that pharmacologically that is not true. Pharmacologically, alcohol is not a stimulant but a depressant; there is no question about that at all. But if you look at a man who takes alcohol you get the impression that it is stimulating him, and people take it in excess because they think it is a stimulant – in a very odd way alcohol does seem to stimulate a person. The immediate effects of alcohol are, secondly, an enhancement of all the faculties; thirdly, joy; fourthly, fellowship. Now you see how, in interpreting the Scriptures we do expose ourselves to misunderstanding from small pedantic minds; it sounds as if I am advocating alcohol because of its effect.[1] In fact, I am simply pointing out to you that alcohol, whether we like it or not, does lead to those effects and it is for these reasons that people partake of it. The man who is nervous drinks, and he is a foolish man for doing so, but he does it because it does help him for the time being – it seems to

---

[1] Dr Lloyd-Jones did not himself drink alcohol.

enhance his faculties.

Furthermore, people drink when they want to be happy. They find life with its cares and problems very trying and depressing, so they take alcohol and it makes them feel happy. There is no question about it – they do, for a time, feel happy, but they fail to realise the terrible risk they are running of still more depression. They take it because it promotes an immediate sense of joy and fellowship; it is one of the most pathetic things of life at the present time that men and women are so unhappy and self-centred that the vast majority seem to find it impossible to have fellowship with others without the help of drink. They have to drink and drug themselves before they get on with one another! Drink, they say, makes them convivial, they are not convivial without it, and thereby they are attesting to the fact that one of the effects of alcohol is to give this sense of good fellowship.

Those, then, are in general the effects of wine or alcohol, and Scripture states this many times. The psalmist spoke about wine which 'maketh glad the heart of man' (Ps 104:15). So now we must take all this and apply it in terms of the work of the Holy Spirit upon us, when he is controlling us. Quite clearly, you cannot read the book of the Acts or the New Testament epistles without seeing that on the surface the analogy is very close. Here are some of the effects upon these disciples and apostles of being filled with the Spirit. First and foremost, they had a clearer understanding of truth. Look at it in the Gospels. There is the greatest teacher the world has ever known. He speaks the word to them, but they stumble at it, and cannot understand it. They do not know what it is all about. But then they are filled with the Spirit and they understand the Scriptures. Listen to Peter preaching on the Day of Pentecost; he expounded the Scriptures and he had a clear understanding of them. It was the Holy Spirit who enabled him to do it. His faculties had been enhanced, and he saw things clearly – the Holy Spirit always does that. Then the disciples also had great joy in the Scriptures, and, furthermore, they clearly had power to explain and preach the word of God and to deliver it. All this was the effect of the Holy Spirit, and as a result of that one sermon by Peter on the Day of Pentecost three thousand souls were converted. It was not Peter, but the Holy Spirit. The word went to the conscience of the hearers, it disturbed them and they were converted. They cried out, 'Men and brethren, what shall we do?' (Acts 2:37) – that is the power that the Holy Spirit gives to a man when he fills him. The man is above himself – you cannot explain him in terms of himself.

But did you notice, too, the boldness that it gave them? Alcohol seems to do that also, which is why it is wrong for a man who has been drinking to drive a car. He seems to have a daring and a boldness. This, again, is all wrong pharmacologically, but we are looking at it generally, and we can understand it, because a man under the influence of alcohol loses his nervousness. And we see the parallel in the New Testament. In Acts we see Peter, who a few days before had denied his Lord three times because he was afraid, now standing before a huge crowd in Jerusalem, and even when confronted by the Sanhedrin saying boldly, 'Whether it be right in the sight of God to hearken unto you more than unto God, judge ye. For we cannot but speak the things which we have seen and heard' (Acts 4:19-20). He had boldness in witness and in testimony, and was ready to suffer anything for the sake of his blessed Lord. Indeed, all the disciples had a boldness which they had never known before, desiring to witness and then witnessing. And then there was the remarkable joy that came into their lives, a joy that nothing could hinder or control. You see the closeness of the analogy? These men were rendered immune to circumstances. They were quite impervious to the things that were said of them, and done to them. There is that glorious example of Paul and Silas in the prison at Philippi, praying and singing praises to God, even though their feet were held fast in the stocks and their poor backs were sore from being scourged and lashed by the jailers. Later, Paul wrote to the Philippian converts, 'Rejoice in the Lord alway' (Phil 4:4). And this they did, even when they were thrown to the lions in the arena; they thanked God they had been counted worthy to suffer shame for his name's sake. It was a joy which was irrepressible, that nothing could quench, and it was all the result of being filled with the Spirit.

Then there was the fruit of the Spirit in their lives: love, joy, peace, longsuffering, meekness, and so on: as you look at these men and women and read about them, you can see those characteristics exemplified in their lives. For when people are filled with the Spirit they do show these things – they cannot help it. The Spirit is controlling them is the Spirit of love; they become like Christ himself, who was filled with the Spirit.

And then another great characteristic was a wonderful sense of thankfulness to the Lord, and a love of the Lord. Having received the enlightenment of the Spirit, they loved the Lord and were grateful to him. They could not do too much for him. The first thing Paul said to the Lord when he saw him on the road to Damascus was, ' Lord, what wilt thou have me to do?' because he knew this sense of thankfulness and of gratitude.

And the last thing I would note is their sense of true fellowship together, their love for one another, and the way in which they felt they belonged to one another. There was no stiffness among them. They did not stand on ceremony, neither did they hold themselves at a distance from one another lest they give themselves away. There was freedom and they mixed with one another, they sang together, they prayed together and they enjoyed one another's fellowship and society. There was no distinction of class or order, nor of wealth or poverty; in all these things they all became one. This amazing unity was present because they had come to see that they were all sinners; they were all equally failures in the sight of God, and all other distinctions were irrelevant and unimportant. They were all filled with the same Spirit; Jew and Gentile no longer existed since they were, now, all one in Christ, having access by one Spirit unto the Father.

Those, then, are some of the results of being filled with the Spirit, and you see how similar they are to the effects of alcohol, and the closeness of the analogy . But let me hurry to point out the contrast between the two. It is that the way of alcohol leads ultimately to an excess, which you can translate by the word riot, or lack of control, and finally to a moral wreckage. Paul's injunction is, 'Be not drunk with wine, wherein is excess' – this disorder and confusion – but, rather, 'be filled with the Spirit.' 'At first,' says the Apostle in effect, 'they seem alike, and yet how different they are!' When it is the work of the Holy Spirit, all these things that I have just been enumerating are under perfect control.

The Scripture is full of this. Did you notice how Paul immediately illustrates what he means by this difference? 'Be not drunk with wine, wherein is excess; but be filled with the Spirit ...' Then, still the same sentence, 'speaking to yourselves in psalms and hymns and spiritual songs, singing and making melody in your heart to the Lord; giving thanks always for all things unto God and the Father in the name of our Lord Jesus Christ.' That is the happiness produced by the Spirit. It is a holy happiness which expresses itself in that way. But then he goes on in verse 21 to put it like this: 'Submitting yourselves one to another in the fear of God' – there is no lack of control there. Wine produces lack of control, and some people's conception of being filled with the Spirit obviously suggests the same thing, but here there is control: submitting yourselves one to another in the fear of the Lord. You realise you are in the presence of God. Certainly, you are filled with joy, you are filled with the Spirit, but everything you do is in the fear of the Lord. Your joy is immense, and some people think that that means riot and confusion. Not at all! We are still in the presence of God, whom we must always approach with reverence and godly fear.

Let me give you some other examples and demonstrations of this truth. The classic passage on this subject is 1 Corinthians 14. It is there that Paul shows us clearly that to be filled with the Spirit means control. Take, for example, verse 14, where he is talking of speaking with tongues: 'For if I pray in an unknown tongue, my spirit prayeth, but my understanding is unfruitful'; and then in verse 15 he says, 'What is it then? I will pray with the spirit, and I will pray with the understanding also: I will sing with the spirit, and I will sing with the understanding also.' Verses 18 and 19 add: 'I thank my God, I speak with tongues more than ye all: yet in the church I had rather speak five words with my understanding, that by my voice I might teach others also, than ten thousand words in an unknown tongue.' He preferred to speak five words with his understanding than ten thousand words in an unknown tongue, in order that he might teach others also.

Then there is the famous exhortation, 'in understanding be men' (1 Cor 14:20), not children but adults, grown up, so that you have a true understanding. Next, Paul says quite categorically in verse 32, 'The spirits of the prophets are subject to the prophets.' I once met a man who could not control himself, he could not restrain himself from calling out in meetings. He was ruining services by his interjections, and of course he thought he was filled with the Spirit, and was appreciating truth. On my speaking and appealing to him he said, 'I cannot help it, I am filled with the Spirit. I am a prophet.' But then I pointed out to him that the Scripture says that the spirits of the prophets are subject to the prophets. Paul says that you must only speak one at a time, and if you see somebody else is giving a message you sit down, and, again, you do not speak in tongues unless there is someone to interpret. The Scriptures teach order. Indeed, Paul sums it up in verse 33 by saying, 'For God is not the author of confusion, but of peace, as in all churches of the saints.' He is always the author of peace and not of confusion.

Finally, he says in verse 40, 'Let all things be done decently and in order.' He is talking about public services and he visualises a stranger coming in and wanting to know what it is all about. The stranger will think you are all mad, says Paul, unless there is control and discipline. Certainly, be filled with the Spirit, but that does not mean you have lost control of yourselves. Rather, it means having a good understanding, this amazing control of the Spirit. As Paul again puts it in 2 Timothy 1:7, 'For God hath not given us the spirit of fear, but of power, and of love, and of a sound mind.' The Spirit is the Spirit of power and love and, at the same time, of control and discipline.

There, then, is what is meant in the Scriptures by being filled with the Spirit. I have tried to put the two sides, the positive and the negative. I have no doubt at all but that for many of us it is hardly necessary that I should emphasise the similarities and the contrasts, for there is not much danger of our giving way to excess and riot! Indeed, I fear our tendency is the exact opposite. Are we filled with the Spirit? Have we got this clear understanding? Do we know anything about this joy? Do we know anything about a holy boldness? Do we *really* know the fellowship? That is the question! These are always the results of being filled with the Spirit. Is there a deep sense of thankfulness to God and Christ in our hearts? These are the manifestations of the Spirit, and the proofs of our being filled with the Spirit.

Let us examine ourselves, my friends. Merely to be decent and controlled, does not mean being filled with the Spirit – all these aspects of the Spirit have to be taken together, for there is a kind of polarity about them. The Christian is the man who seems to be always walking on a knife edge: there is ever the danger of excess, yet he does not give way to it, because he is controlled. It is this perfect balance. He is controlled by the Holy Spirit. It was the Spirit who brought order into chaos in the world at the beginning and he has always been the Spirit of order, but the two things must go together. There is a difference between order and lack of life; there is no disorder among the dead. But the truth before us is the order of the living. It is control of power, fear of God and a sound mind.

So I trust that we shall start examining ourselves and asking if there is something about us that at first might lead men to think that perhaps we are under the influence of wine. Is there something exalted and free; is there a sense of power; is there a sense of knowledge; is there a sense of almost being possessed; is there something about us that makes people feel we are not ordinary people? That is always true of those who are filled with the Spirit. They do not have to drag themselves wearily to God's house, nor do they have to force themselves to try to be Christian, and to behave as such. No, they are controlled by the Holy Spirit.

Those are the characteristics, the manifestations, and the results of being filled with the Spirit. Oh that we were all such people! Oh that the first reaction of anybody meeting us, the first thing they sensed, was something unusual, some strange power, some strange peace and joy and equanimity, the fruit of the Spirit, something suggesting the Lord Jesus Christ himself! 'Be not drunk with wine, wherein is excess; but be filled with the Spirit.'

8

Controlled by the Spirit

And be not drunk with wine, wherein is excess; but be filled with the Spirit (Ephesians 5:18).

We have been considering together Paul's injunction to us to be filled with the Spirit, and so obviously the great question for us to consider is how this can be true of us. How are we to become the kind of person delineated in the New Testament – rejoicing in Christ Jesus, filled with love and joy and peace and all these other manifestations of the gracious work of the Spirit? In order to consider that, we come back again to this verse in Ephesians, and there are a number of preliminary points to which I must call your attention. In the first place, we notice that this is a command: 'Be not drunk with wine, wherein is excess; but *be filled* with the Spirit,' and then, secondly, we see that it is a continuous command. It really means '*go on* being filled' with the Spirit. Paul does not tell us to be filled with the Spirit once, and from then on to live on this great gift we have received. Rather, the command is that we should be constantly filled with the Spirit, it is a continuous performance. And the last general point I would make in this connection is that the verb is in the passive – it says, 'go on *being* filled'. It does not say, 'go on filling yourselves with the Spirit', because that is patently something we cannot do. Now that is important. It is a reminder again that the Holy Spirit is a Person; so that we cannot, as it were, fill ourselves with the Holy Spirit whenever we like. But what we can do is allow the

Holy Spirit to fill us – we can go on being filled with him; it is a command, a continuous command, and in the passive.

Now there is a good deal of confusion in people's minds with respect to the way in which we can reconcile these two – the command and the passive element. There are two main schools of thought with regard to this, as there generally are with regard to all these matters. They both take their case to different extremes, whereas scriptural teaching combines the two. As I have just said, it seems to me that the only way of holding these two ideas comfortably in our minds at one and the same time is to take a firm hold of the fact that the Holy Spirit is a Person. We must therefore, as we have seen, cease to think in terms of some power, like electricity, or some liquid being poured into us, like some kind of force or energy. Rather, because the Holy Spirit is a Person, then the essence of being filled with the Spirit is that our lives should be consciously controlled by him.

What exactly, therefore, does this involve? 'That,' someone may say, 'is what I desire above everything else, but how does it happen? What do I have to do?' Let us start again with the negative: there is no teaching in the Scriptures that tells us that what we have to do is wait or agonise in prayer for this to happen to us. Nor must we allow ourselves to go into a state of complete passivity, neither in the form known as 'tarrying' nor in any other form. There are some people who do not teach the tarrying, but who do teach complete passivity. They would say that if we want to be filled with the Spirit we must just cease from action altogether and even from thinking; and that the whole art in this matter is the art of abandonment, of resignation, an attempt, as it were, to annihilate our very personalities and to surrender ourselves in that complete sense.

But here, again, I suggest that that is a teaching which cannot be substantiated from the New Testament. If that teaching were true, then we would find that all Christians were identical and there would be no manifestations of individuality and personality whatsoever in any teacher or preacher. That, however, is clearly not the case; the apostle Paul retained his essential personality, so did the apostle Peter. People have fallen into the same error with regard to the inspiration of the Scriptures, but here again, personality remains, and the styles of writing of the apostle Peter and the apostle John are entirely different, although the message is the same and it is all perfectly controlled by the Holy Spirit. Thus, it is surely obvious that to be filled with the Spirit does not mean a kind of mechanical passivity, with a man's personality going out of action – it is something much more wonderful than that. It means, rather, that though the man's personality is still there it is entirely controlled by the Holy Spirit – that is the principle.

Perhaps the best way I can put this to you is to put it in terms of the supreme example of it, and that is none other than the Lord Jesus Christ himself. I wonder whether we have grasped this as we should? It is indeed one of the most astounding things in the Scriptures – it is certainly the essence of understanding the Incarnation and all that followed. We are told two things about the Lord Jesus Christ which on the surface seem to be quite incompatible. Firstly, we are told that he is very God of very God. While he lived here on earth, he was still the eternal Son of God, not in any way shorn of any of the powers that were his in heaven. He did not divest himself of his godhead; he was still God in the fullest sense conceivable. Yet we are told about him that he was baptised with the Holy Spirit, that the Holy Spirit descended upon him, and John tells us that 'God giveth not the Spirit by measure unto him' (Jn 3:34). We are also told that he was filled with the Spirit and led of the Spirit. Indeed, he himself says things like this – he, the very eternal Son of God, co–equal, co–eternal with God but undiminished in his power, he says, 'As my Father hath taught me, I speak these things' (Jn 8:28). He says that all his words and all his works are given to him by his Father. He is told what to say, and he is told what to do. He says, 'I seek not mine own will, but the will of the Father which hath sent me' (Jn 5:30).

How do we understand all this? How do we reconcile these statements with one another? Surely the answer must be that the Lord Jesus Christ, the eternal Son of God, having taken unto himself human nature and having appeared, therefore, in 'the likeness of sinful flesh' as a man, deliberately took upon himself the form of a servant, and subjected himself and his own personality to the leading and the guidance of the Spirit. He did not do away with his personality, nor even with his gifts, but he chose, for the sake of our salvation, to humble himself in that way. He did not exercise his own will, nor did he depend upon his own power, in order to achieve our redemption, but lived life as a man. So, while all these powers and faculties and propensities were there, he did not exercise them, but was dependent and subservient to the Father and the Holy Spirit. Thus we find ourselves confronted by the whole marvel and miracle of the Incarnation and his life here upon earth – that he, who had created all things and by whom all things consist, seemed to be entirely dependent, weak and helpless. The explanation is that he willed all this, quite deliberately. He submitted himself to this control and leading.

When you and I are exhorted and commanded to be filled with the Spirit it means exactly the same thing. We are to do, in turn, what the Son of God did when he was here on earth. We are to realise that the Holy Spirit is within us, and we are to realise what his desire is with respect to us. We put that earlier in terms of James 4:5, 'that the spirit' that God has caused to dwell within us 'lusteth to envy' for our sanctification – the 'flesh lusteth against the Spirit, and the Spirit against the flesh' (Gal 5:17). His supreme desire is that we may be sanctified and holy, that we may really be separated from the world, and unto God. We must realise that and submit to him, allowing him to do his work within us. We must know something of his great power within us, that he is working within us 'both to will and to do of his good pleasure'. Therefore, that is obviously the essential principle in this matter. We must submit ourselves to his control in all things, and that is the essence of this command to be filled with the Spirit.

But I know that having said that I am still leaving large numbers of people in difficulty with regard to how exactly these two things can be put together. How can I, living my life in the flesh, manifest the personality which God has given me, and yet at the same time be subservient to the power of the Holy Spirit and be led and controlled by him? What exactly is our relationship to the Spirit? At this point people generally use illustrations and there is no doubt that a picture or analogy can be of value. Yet I think we must always be very careful with illustrations. If I venture to put one to you now, in order to make this point clear, I realise that I am doing something that is attended by considerable risk; for no one illustration can convey the whole truth, though different illustrations may perhaps represent different aspects of the matter. There are two illustrations that are very frequently used which seem to me to be quite wrong and utterly misleading. The first illustration which is used is this. Imagine a man in the sea or in a pool of water. 'Now,' it is said, 'the body of that man has a tendency to sink and will probably do so, for that is the natural thing to do – to go down. But,' they continue, 'if that man puts a lifebelt on he will no longer sink, because the lifebelt holds him up.' So, according to that illustration, our Lord, through the Holy Spirit, is, as it were, a kind of lifebelt that keeps us from sinking. That, therefore, is the way not to sin and to be sanctified and to live the holy life: you abide in Christ, you put on the lifebelt and the lifebelt will hold you up. But the difficulty with that illustration, it seems to me, is that it suggests utter passivity: all you do is don your lifebelt; indeed, they go so far as to say that the moment you are out of the lifebelt, down you go.

Then another illustration used by the same people is the famous illustration about the poker. The poker is black and cold and rigid, but if you take it and put it into a fire it will become hot and you will be able to bend it. While it remains in the fire it is red hot, but the moment you take it out it becomes cold and black and rigid again. So the only thing you have to do is to see that the poker is kept in the fire, because while it is there, the fire will do all these things to it and for it. Once again, I suggest that that is a representation of pure passivity and for this reason those two illustrations have never commended themselves to me. So I would venture to put to you some other pictures. I remind you again that I am well aware of the defects of all illustrations, but

I am trying to take spiritual teaching a little further and it seems to me that a figure like this surely does help at this point.

Imagine a man starting up a business – it does not matter what sort, take a grocer's, if you like. There is the man, working in that business, weighing up his pounds of sugar and doing the things that have to be done. He is, of course, doing his best, working as hard as he can, because the harder he works the more business he gets, and his bank balance is going to show the result. However, for various reasons this man decides to sell this one-man owned business to a company, to a chain store. But a part of the agreement is that he should stay on in the same shop as manager. The position now is that that man, in the self-same shop, should be doing exactly what he did before. He should be equally careful, equally zealous, equally polite, equally anxious to attract business, equally careful in his weighing. Yet there is this obvious difference – he is no longer doing it for himself, and at the back of it all he is being controlled by another power who can step in at any time and suggest various things to him. Beforehand, he decided everything, now he is subservient to another authority, to which he submits. He does all he can, he is not passive, he is going on as he was before and yet he is being controlled. The control of the business, its ultimate prosperity, success and profit are not in his hands. As a result, at one and the same time, the man's individuality and personality are pre-served absolutely and yet he is being controlled by this com-pany, by this higher power.

That is one illustration, and yet it seems to me that there is a difficulty about it which I must correct by giving you another. It does not represent the power that works *within* us. It deals with the question of control, and of the relationship of wills, but it does not show that over and above the Holy Spirit is within us, working within us both to will and to do. This is the ultimate guarantee of our being sanctified and living the holy life.

So I must take a second illustration, which is perhaps a little more difficult and involved. Yet it is very helpful to me person-ally, and so I want to suggest it to you. Let us try to look at this in terms of a man who is subject to seasickness, sailing on a boat.

Now this man's desire is to avoid being seasick. There is one method that is advocated for dealing with this which, from the standpoint of physiology, is very sound, and which has the advantage of being successful in practice, and it is this. The man is told first and foremost to stand as far forward as he can upon the ship. Then he is told that at all costs he must not look at the waves, nor at the side of the ship nor immediately in front of him. Even though everything within him wants to do this, it is the one thing he must not do; instead, he must look at the horizon in the far distance. Not only must he avert his gaze from the waves, he must also look at the horizon, and, furthermore, he must deliberately try not to balance himself, he must relax completely.

Now the reason why the man is told to do this is that there is a mechanism in our bodies, in what is called the inner ear, which is especially put there by God to keep us in a balanced condition; a wonderful little mechanism called the semi-circular canals. This mechanism is most intricate, but as long as we can relax, it will work. We must avoid doing anything that makes us think about it, in order to give these semi-circular canals a chance to do the work which they have been put into our body to do. We must also avoid the things that makes us feel sick, but though we may keep all these rules about diet, yet if we still keep looking at the waves we will probably be ill. So we keep all those rules, we avoid looking at the waves, and trying to balance ourselves, and holding ourselves rigid. We let these semi-circular canals in our body do their work, and if we do this we will find that we will not suffer from seasickness.

There, it seems to me, we have a very helpful analogy. You have perhaps been told by sailors and others that for the first few days at sea they are generally seasick but, they say, it passes and they are all right again. What happens is that unconsciously they get into the way of doing all the things which I have been describing to you. We talk about 'the rolling gait' of the typical sailor; it is because he has got into the habit of rolling backwards and forwards with the ship. He is allowing the mechanism of the body to maintain his balance. Now for all its imperfections,

I suggest to you that this illustration again points to something that is being taught by the Scriptures. The Holy Spirit is in us. He is there to do this work, so we must let him do it. But it is not a complete passivity on our part because there is a great deal which we have to do. Even though the Holy Spirit is in us, if we keep looking at the world and its enticements and attractions, we will go down. So what we must do is realise God's provision for us in this respect and co-operate with him. We must work with the Spirit, and as long as we are working with the Spirit, and carrying out these instructions, we shall not be fulfilling the lusts of the flesh.

Those, then, are two pictures which I have offered for your consideration in order to illustrate certain things which are stated so clearly in the Scriptures. Listen, for instance, to the apostle Paul. When dealing with this subject he almost seems to be contradicting himself, but there is no contradiction if you remember the principle – 'I can do all things through Christ which strengtheneth me' (Phil 4:13). You see the apparent contradiction? There was once an old-style preacher, who kept on saying over and over again, 'I can do all things …' Then he put a question to the Apostle and said, 'Paul, do you mean to say you can do this and that?'

'Yes,' said Paul, 'I can do it.'

So the preacher came to the conclusion that Paul was a great egoist who was always boasting, and he was very doubtful whether Paul really could do all the things of which he boasted. But Paul kept on saying, 'I can do all things' – and then he went on to say, 'I can do all things *through Christ which strengtheneth me.*'

'I beg your pardon,' said the old preacher, 'I did not realise there were two of you!'

That is so characteristic of the Scriptures. I can indeed do all things. I am the one who does them, but in a sense I am only doing them because of this higher control. I can do all things through Christ who strengthens me, by means of the power which he is giving me through his Holy Spirit. I cannot do them alone, but I do them because of the way in which he enables me to do them. I am not passive, but active, as we see also in Galatians 2:20. Notice how Paul goes on, each thing seeming to contradict the one before, but there is no contradiction at all. What Paul is saying, in effect, is this: 'I am no longer living for myself; I am now submitting myself to and am controlled by the Holy Spirit. I am doing this deliberately, I am subjecting myself.' How zealous he was! He worked harder than any other preacher, 'more than them all', as he constantly says, and yet he is not boasting because it is all being done after, and according to, the life of the Spirit.

But perhaps the final example of this is the one which we find running through the Old Testament. The whole trouble with the children of Israel was that they failed to realise this particular principle which we are considering together. That is what God keeps on saying to them: 'Why do you not listen to me? You do not realise who you are and what you are! They constantly failed to realise that they were God's people. They forgot that if they would but realise that, if they would only keep in the right relationship to him, they would have nothing to worry about at all. Look at the amazing way in which God routed their enemies. He had promised to do that and he used the children of Israel to accomplish it, but they kept on forgetting, and kept comparing themselves with the other nations. 'We must have a king,' they said, 'because the other nations have one.' They could not trust God, so they had a human, earthly king. And then they saw other nations making alliances in order to defend their territories, and they said that they must do the same; so they made alliances with the Syrians and others. Then they said that others were using horses, so they must use them too. All along, their trouble was due to the fact that they did not realise who they were, what God's promises were and the power of his might.

'Let me be your rear-guard,' says God in effect. 'Let me be your horsemen and your horses and your chariots. I can be, I will be – trust me, co-operate with me. Do all that you are doing by my power and by my strength. Let me work in you and through you.'

It was because they constantly failed to realise that teaching that they went so frequently and so sadly astray.

So there we have what, it seems to me, is the essential principle in this great matter – this relationship between myself and the Spirit, my will and his will; how at one and the same time I can say that I do something and yet that he does it. Think of it supremely in terms of our Lord himself and the way he lived his life as a man here in this world, dependent upon the Father for words, for works, for everything. And you and I are to realise that God has put his Spirit within us. We must listen to him and be attracted to him and be controlled by him and work with him as he enables us. Again, we must turn to Paul's great statement in Philippians: 'Work out your own salvation with fear and trembling. For it is God which worketh in you both to will and to do of his good pleasure.'

There is the principle, and having laid that down, we are now in a position to proceed to the practical instructions that are given. If all this is true in essence, this is what I must remember: I must never grieve the Spirit, and, positively, I must walk in the Spirit.

9

The Temple of the Holy Spirit

Walk in the Spirit, and ye shall not fulfil the lust of the flesh (Galatians 5:16).

And grieve not the holy Spirit of God (Ephesians 4:30).

We are in the process of considering what is meant by the command, 'Be filled with the Spirit.' Having seen that it means to be controlled by the Person of the Spirit, who is at work in all Christians, we tried, in chapter 8, to rid our minds of the confusion which so often exists in the matter of how we reconcile our wills with the will of the Spirit. We saw that we can easily slip into a false passivity and fail to give due weight to the various exhortations of the Bible. Now clearly the Scriptures do not tell us that we have nothing to do, indeed they address many negative injunctions to us. The Apostle tells the Ephesians, for instance, that they are not to steal any longer, that no corrupt communication is to proceed out of their mouth, that they are to cleanse themselves from all filthiness of the flesh and of the mind, and that they are to avoid fornication and all uncleanness or covetousness, or foolish talking and jesting. All these things we are told to refrain from; but at the same time the Scriptures teach that we are to work out our own salvation with fear and trembling because God works in us, and we illustrated this by a number of analogies.

So, having considered this in general, let us now round off

this matter by coming down to a more practical aspect; because it is not enough merely to grasp the principles, we must know something of what this means in detail – how am I to be filled with the Spirit? We have already got rid of the idea of just being filled in the sense that a vessel is filled by liquid being poured into it. As we saw, it is not merely receiving a force, or a power, or energy, but rather a question of being controlled and led by this Person, the Holy Spirit. That is the key to the understanding of the practical aspect of this matter, and I suggested, at the end of the last study, that we must bear in mind the two main things which are taught in the Scriptures themselves. The first is that there are certain things which we must avoid. Now the Bible is very careful to call our attention to this. Three different terms are used in this connection. First, we are told that when Stephen preached to the people, he said, 'You do always resist the Holy Ghost ...' (Acts 7:51). Then you find in 1 Thessalonians 5:19 the injunction: 'Quench not the Spirit'; and, thirdly, in Ephesians 4:30 Paul says, 'Grieve not the holy Spirit of God.'

Those are the three great negative injunctions with regard to this matter, but it seems to me that for practical purposes the only one we need to concern ourselves with is the third. The first about 'resisting' the Spirit was addressed to unbelievers, and I think that it is a term that is always more applicable to an unbeliever than it is to a believer. The one who resists the operation of the Spirit is the unbeliever, and I would say that a believer cannot resist the Holy Spirit in that sense. Then the second term about 'quenching' the Spirit has reference not so much to the individual and his not being filled with the Spirit, but rather to the conduct of public services. If you read the context in 1 Thessalonians 5, you will find that it has reference to what Christian people do to other Christians. Its whole context concerns prophecy and manifesting the various gifts of the Spirit, and the Christians in Thessalonica are exhorted not to quench the Spirit in his operations and manifestations in a public service in the church of God. So, strictly speaking, I think it is wrong to appropriate that term about quenching the Spirit to this whole matter of Christians individually being filled with the

Spirit, although, of course, there is a sense in which it does come in.

But the third injunction really includes everything. So that if we are thinking of being filled with the Spirit, the negative term that we must bear in mind is that we are exhorted not to grieve him. Now Paul puts that statement right in the midst of a great ethical exhortation to the Ephesians: 'Let no corrupt communication proceed out of your mouth, but that which is good to the use of edifying, that it may minister grace unto the hearers. And grieve not the holy Spirit of God, whereby ye are sealed unto the day of redemption.' Then immediately – 'Let all bitterness and wrath, and anger, and clamour, and evil speaking, be put away from you, with all malice: and be ye kind one to another, tenderhearted, forgiving one another, even as God for Christ's sake hath forgiven you.'

What, then, does this mean in practice? How are we to avoid grieving the Spirit? Now the very terms, it seems to me, suggest the answer. Take the very word 'grieve', for instance, a word which at once conveys to us the sensitive character of the Spirit. He is compared to a dove and he came more than once in the semblance of a dove, suggesting again his gentle, sensitive character. The Holy Spirit, if one may speak with reverence, never forces himself upon us. He is a Person and one who has those particular characteristics. If, therefore, we are anxious to be filled with the Spirit – which means being controlled and directed by him – then obviously the first thing which we must bear in mind is that in view of his character we must be careful not to grieve or offend him in any way. Still more, we must remember what his object is and what his desires are. We must never lose sight of the fact that the Holy Spirit is primarily concerned about our sanctification. He is in us, and, as James reminds us, he is 'lusting even unto envy' for our sanctification. He wants to draw us from the world and to separate us unto God. He is working in us to do that. Therefore, if we want him to have his way, we must be very careful not to grieve him.

How, then, do we grieve him? I am coming right down to the practical aspects of this question because every single item is of extreme importance. This will not be an exhaustive list, but here are some of the most important aspects of the matter. We grieve the Spirit, first of all, by forgetting him altogether and entirely ignoring his existence. Here we are confronted by the extraordinary fact that through Christ God has given us the gift of the Spirit. When our Lord had finished his work on earth, when he had gone through death and had borne our sins, when he had vanquished death and the grave, and had ascended to heaven and there taken his seat at the right hand of God, in view of all that he had done, God gave him the gift of the Spirit to give to his people and he has given us that gift. Yet we are so often entirely oblivious of that fact. We do not realise it, we do not stop to consider it. We fail to realise as we should the fact that the Holy Spirit is within us.

Now some of those members of the church at Corinth, to whom we have already referred, those people who had believed that Christ had died for them, clearly did not realise that they were guilty of sins; and Paul says to them, 'Know ye not that your bodies are the temples of the Holy Spirit which is in you?' (1 Cor 6:19). You are grieving him, acting and behaving as if this were not a fact, says Paul, and that is why you are in trouble. There is nothing more insulting to a person than to forget or ignore him. To pretend that you have not seen people is the supreme way of insulting them. You are walking along the street and you do not want to see someone, so you just pass him or her by – you cannot insult anybody more than by behaving like that. And yet, my friends, is not that the way we all of us tend to treat the Holy Spirit? To forget him for a moment is to grieve and insult him, and we are called upon to avoid doing this above everything else. The thing is unthinkable, and yet how frequently we behave in that way. Whatever you and I may do, the Holy Spirit is within us and he knows it all. He who is the guest within us is with us in every action and every thought, and nothing is more terrible than to forget and ignore him entirely.

Next, we ignore the Spirit by neglecting his word. The Bible, the word of God, is the work of the Holy Spirit – we have agreed about that. It is his book, written not merely by men, but by men who were inspired and moved, borne and carried along, by the Holy Spirit: 'Holy men spake as they were moved by the Holy Ghost' (2 Pet 1:21). The Bible is the special work of the Holy Spirit. He is really the author of the book, and he has given it to us in order that we may learn what to avoid and what to do: so that we may be sanctified – 'Sanctify them through thy truth: thy word is truth.' Thus, if there is one thing of which we can always be absolutely certain, it is that the Holy Spirit is always guiding us to this book. It is his way of leading and directing us. He does not only lead us directly, but indirectly also, and particularly through this word. Obviously, therefore, we are grieving the Spirit if we do not study the Bible as he means us to, if we are not regular in our reading of it, or if we do not grow in our knowledge of it. Now there are many people in that position. You will often find it in discussions. You talk about a certain subject and ask how a certain problem can be solved, and you find that there are large numbers of people who regard themselves as entirely scriptural and yet say that they pray to the Spirit to guide them. But that should be quite unnecessary, because if they went to the Bible, they would find the answer to their question! It is not honouring him to ignore the word and to go directly to him, because he has already given us the answer there. The Bible is the word of the Spirit and he works in it and through it. Indeed, there are some who would say he only guides us in that way, but that, I think, is going too far. However, I would go so far as to say that his normal way of working is to guide and direct us through the word.

Once more I would commend to you a study of this matter as it is to be found in the history of the Puritans of the seventeenth century; such a study is most instructive. The great division that took place within the Puritan movement, with the Quakers on the one side, and men like Dr John Owen on the other, was on this very subject. The tendency of the Quaker was to say that he did not need the word but that the Spirit did everything for him in the 'inner light', by operating directly upon his mind. So they tended to depreciate the word, which is clearly wrong. But we must not go as far as the Puritans went and say it is the *only* way. The true balance is to realise that this is the *normal* way. Thank God that that is so, because if we are without the word because of circumstances, the Spirit can deal with us directly and he does so.

The next way we should avoid grieving the Spirit is that we must never be in any doubt or unbelief concerning the purposes and the desires of the Holy Spirit within us; and still less must we ever doubt his ability to help us. I take it that we all know what I mean by that. It is one thing to believe these things theoretically, it is quite another to believe them in actual practice. Do we really rely upon the power of the Spirit within us, or do we doubt it? Do we still harbour a certain amount of unbelief? Are we all perfectly certain that God has given us his Spirit, in order that his great purpose of sanctification in us may be brought to pass? Are we quite sure that the power of the Spirit is really sufficient and that it matters not at all what the problem is, nor how powerful the enemy, for the Spirit that is in us is greater than that which is in them? The apostle John says to his young followers, You need not be afraid. I know all about the world, the flesh and the devil. I know its subtlety, but I assure you, 'Greater is he that is in you, than he that is in the world' (1 Jn 4:4). The power that is in us is greater, and let us never forget it. We must be grieving the Holy Spirit terribly when we doubt his sufficiency. Furthermore – I am going to say something now that can be misunderstood, but it is the teaching of the Scriptures – as Christians, we must not be afraid of ourselves. That does not mean we are self-confident; because self-confidence is not a fruit of the Spirit. But we are told not to be frightened of the devil in the sense of being afraid of temptations. Rather, we are told to resist him in the faith. I must have this element of confidence in the ability and the power of the Holy Spirit within me.

But that leads me on to another terrible way of grieving the Spirit, and I can sum it up in one word: 'self'. I suppose this is the way in which we grieve him most of all – when we elevate self in the place of the Spirit. I cannot think of a better way of illustrating this than to go back again to what I have reminded you concerning our Lord in his earthly life. Paul puts it in that great sentence: 'Let this mind be in you, which was also in Christ Jesus' (Phil 2:5). What sort of a mind was that? We are told that he was one who 'made himself of no reputation' (v. 7). In other words, he did not think of himself, but submitted himself. He always submitted to the will of his Father, to the will of the Spirit, and you and I are to do the same. Self-will in a Christian means grieving the Spirit. He wants us to submit our wills to his, to co-operate with him and to be led by him. Not that we become passive machines but, rather, we put our wills into his, and, having submitted ourselves, we then exercise our wills because they now conform to his. My illustration of the man in business applies here again. He is working as hard as he can, yes, but for a new management, not for himself. So any manifestation of self is grieving to the Spirit. If I want my way, my rights, my will, if I am sensitive about myself and my reputation, I must be grieving the Spirit, for all manifestations of self are grieving to him.

Then I go on to the next point, which is sin in all forms. It does not matter what form it takes – thoughts, imaginations, desires, lusts, passions and all wrong actions – sin is always grieving to the Spirit. We can sum this up by saying that anything which is not Christian, or which is opposed to the fruit of the Spirit, is a grief to the Spirit. Paul has put it so clearly in Galatians 5, in his contrast between the works of the flesh, and the fruit of the Spirit. Anything, in any shape or form, that belongs to the category of the works of the flesh is grieving to the Spirit – 'the flesh lusteth against the Spirit, and the Spirit against the flesh'(Gal 5:17). He is sensitive, tender and gentle, and if you and I could only begin to think of sins in terms of grieving the Spirit, I am sure we would sin much less than we do. As I have often said, the mistake we all make is to think of a particular sin as 'a sin', whereas we should be thinking of it as something that is incompatible with the Spirit within us. It is not so much a matter of doing wrong, as of hurting a Person, and once we begin to think of it in that way, we are 75% on the way to victory over it.

The next thing I would emphasise is that any hesitation about doing the will of the Spirit is obviously very grieving to him. You know what I mean. The Spirit enlightens our conscience, so that when we are tempted we know exactly that any hesitation about doing the will of the Spirit is a source of grief to him. Or, to take it positively, if he has indicated through his word, or in some other way, that you and I are to do something, and we do not want to do it because it hurts our pride or our flesh or our self-esteem, and we hesitate because we want to do something else instead, can anything be more grieving than that? Can anything be more insulting than to question what is clearly the will of the Spirit? We grieve him by so doing.

But let us now consider two final points, to which I attach very great significance. Surely, to be more interested in the power of the Spirit, or in the experiences and gifts which are given by the Spirit than in the Spirit himself, is to grieve and to insult him? I do not think that that needs any elaboration, since obvious illustrations come to the mind. You can never insult people more than by giving them the impression that you are not really interested in them but merely in what they can do for you. Is there anything more hurtful than to feel that we, as people, are not wanted for ourselves, but only for what we can provide? Yet we can very easily drop into that condition with regard to the Holy Spirit. If we desire experiences and gifts and manifestations rather than the Spirit himself, we are insulting him. Oh, how often we are guilty of that! We are anxious for power in preaching, power in our lives, anxious to be able to show certain spectacular things in our experience, but in the meantime the Spirit himself is forgotten, and so we are guilty, oftentimes, of grieving the sensitive, holy, delicate Spirit of God.

But, lastly, I will put it like this: what is the supreme ambition of the Holy Spirit? There can be no doubt of that, we have it so clearly in the Scriptures. The supreme desire and object and ambition of the Holy Spirit is to reveal, to manifest and to glorify, the Lord Jesus Christ. 'He shall not speak of himself ... he shall glorify me,' says Christ (1 Jn 16:13-14), and he has come in order to do that. His supreme work, as we have seen, is to make the Lord Jesus Christ real to us. Therefore, my friends, if we are interested in anything other than a more intimate know-ledge of the Lord Jesus Christ, we are grieving the Spirit. The supreme ambition and object of the Christian should be to know Christ, and how often we forget that, because we are interested in these other things. The peculiar temptation of any preacher is to want power in his preaching, and yet his supreme ambition should not be to become a powerful preacher, but to know the Lord Jesus Christ so intimately that, like the nineteenth-century American missionary George Bowen, he should be able to stand before a congregation of people, and say that the Lord Jesus Christ is more real to him spiritually 'than you people who are sitting on those seats in front of me'. That is it! Of course we need gifts, and power, and victory, of course we need power in preaching, but all those things are means to an end. The supreme desire should be 'that I may know him and the power of his resurrection, and the fellowship of his suffer-ings' (Phil 3:10). What we need to know about each other is not what gifts we have, nor what experiences we get, but how well we know the Lord Jesus Christ. How real is he to us? How inti-mate are we with him? How deep is our personal consciousness of his presence? That is the supreme test of the fullness of the Spirit.

We now turn from the negative aspect, which I have emphasised because it is so important on the practical level. Let me give you some headings on the positive side. For if I do all that to avoid grieving the Spirit, what do I do positively? Again, the directions are simple: I must walk in the Spirit, I must be led by the Spirit. That is how Paul puts it to us in Galatians 5:16: 'Walk in the Spirit, and ye shall not fulfil the lust of the flesh'; and again he says in verse 25: 'If we live in the Spirit, let us also walk in the Spirit.' The other term is 'being led by the Spirit' which means exactly the same thing. How, then, am I to walk in the Spirit? And the answer to that really does come down to two things. If I want to be filled with the Spirit I need not go to tarrying meetings and agonise and fast. No – what I have to do is to realise that he is within me. I must not grieve him, and I must walk in the Spirit and be led by him.

Now, obviously, this means avoiding everything which we have already been considering together, but I do not want to leave it negatively, I want to put it positively as well. Walking in the Spirit means, first of all, that once again I must always remember that the Holy Spirit is a Person, and I must always recognise the fact that this Person is within me. I have ventured in earlier studies to put a simple rule for life to you in this way: it is a very good thing for Christians, the moment they wake up in the morning, to say to themselves, 'I am a child of God'; but I will give you another way of saying that: 'If the Holy Spirit is within me, my body is the temple of the Holy Spirit; I have this gracious guest within me. Wherever I am today, and whatever I may be doing, the Holy Spirit will be with me. I am not alone, I do not live an isolated life. There is nothing that I can do or that can happen to me but that the Holy Spirit is a sharer in it.' If we but walked with that realisation uppermost in our minds, it would transform everything. That is why we must not commit these sins, says Paul, because of the fact that we have this 'gracious, willing guest' within us. Let us concentrate on this, let us take time to do this, especially first thing in the morning, before the world, the flesh and the devil get in. We have to do this because it will not be done for us. We have seen that we must 'take time to be holy', and that is the first thing we must do: remind ourselves that he is within us and that he is a holy Person.

Then the next thing is that we must deliberately desire to be controlled by him. You say to yourself, 'Well, I know from past experience how easy it is to be controlled by my flesh, and by the world. Therefore I desire that this day I am going to be controlled by the Spirit.' For if you do not do that, you will find that before you have gone many minutes into the day, the flesh will be controlling you. You will become irritable with yourself or with somebody else, and the Holy Spirit is being grieved. So we have deliberately to submit ourselves to him and his control. The moment you read that newspaper the world will take control of you unless you are already being controlled by the Holy

Spirit. If your life and flesh determine what you read in the newspaper, it is quite certain that you will go down and you will suffer for it, but if the Spirit is really controlling you, you will not read much of it, nor will you waste much of your time with it, because it is something outside and it has nothing to do with the spiritual life.

The next thing, therefore, is to trust him and to rely upon his work and power within us. This, again, is a deliberate action of our wills. It is not enough to believe in theory that the Holy Spirit is going to use and control me, I have to rely upon that fact, and in all I do and say I must be conscious of the fact that the Holy Spirit is empowering me. If I have submitted myself to him, he will enable me. He it is who enhances my will and power and I must remind myself of that.

I can give you a simple illustration to prove what I mean. Any man who preaches the gospel must start by saying to himself, 'I can never convert anybody, no man can convert another. If men and women are spiritually dead in trespasses and sins, I cannot convert them by preaching, by eloquence, by argument, by logic, or by demonstration. I cannot do it, it is the Spirit alone who can do this.' But yet, at the same time, of course, we know that the Spirit uses all the things I have just mentioned. The Spirit can use eloquence, as he did in the case of the great George Whitefield, the greatest orator this country has ever known. He used his oratory, yes, but Whitefield did not rely upon his oratory; Whitefield relied upon the Spirit, and the moment he did so the Spirit used his oratory. In the same way, the Spirit used the logic of John Wesley, but he could only use John Wesley's logic after Wesley had submitted himself to him and we, too, must do that with the whole of our life.

The next obvious thing to do is to spend much time with the Scriptures. You cannot be reading the word truly without walking in the Spirit. Then I would put prayer, which really means seeking fellowship with God and with the Lord Jesus Christ. To be led of the Spirit, to walk in the Spirit, means that we spend our time seeking that fellowship. 'This is life eternal, that they might know thee the only true God, and Jesus Christ whom thou hast sent' (Jn 17:3). And if you read the lives of all the men throughout the centuries who have been filled with the Spirit, you will find that they spent a great deal of their time in prayer. The Spirit obviously leads us to God and to Christ. He wants us to have this fellowship and communion. He himself, as it were, has this aspect of communion with the blessed eternal Trinity and he brings us into the fellowship and into the communion.

Then I would enforce all this by saying that we must constantly remind ourselves of these things. The trouble with us, as I have already said, is that we do not talk enough to ourselves. We do not preach enough to ourselves; we all ought to be preachers preaching to that congregation that consists of self. Indeed, half the battle is to talk to ourselves about these things. Address yourself, as the psalmist did. He turns to himself and says, 'Why art thou cast down, O my soul? and why art thou disquieted within me? hope thou in God' (Ps 42:11). He is preaching to himself, and we must do the same. We must take time during the day, indeed many times, to recollect these things, to detach ourselves from business affairs and to say, 'Now I am still this person in whom the Holy Spirit resides and I am using my body and mind in the realisation that it is all the temple of the Holy Spirit.'

So let us remind ourselves, let us refresh our memory, and meditate upon all these things, and, above everything else, let us ever keep ourselves in a sensitive condition. You know what I mean by that. You know what it is to feel yourself becoming hard and insensitive. The moment we discover that, we must be drastic. We must keep ourselves sensitive to the movements and the promptings and the guiding of the Holy Spirit. It will mean repentance, it will mean going back to God and confessing our sin, it will mean humbling ourselves – it does not matter what it may mean, but we must keep ourselves in this sensitive spiritual condition so that we may be conscious of his slightest movement, and we are encouraged to do all this by this great assurance of the Apostle: 'Walk in the Spirit, and ye shall not fulfil the lusts of the flesh.'

Thank God it is a positive gospel! The way to avoid sin is to be walking in the Spirit. The way to avoid going down in life and to live on the high level is to walk in the Spirit, to be led by the Spirit, to meditate upon these things, to be controlled entirely by him. Are we filled with the Spirit? Are we manifesting the fruit of the Spirit? Do we know the joy and the happiness and the peace that the Holy Spirit alone can give? Are we attractive Christians? Do we give people the impression that the most marvellous thing in the world is to be a Christian and to have the Spirit of God within us? This is the thing to which we are called and the way to do that is positively to avoid grieving the Spirit, and to walk in him, to dwell in him as he dwells in us, and to be led by him in all things. 'Be not drunk with wine, wherein is excess; but be filled with the Spirit.'

10

The Wiles of the Devil

Finally, my brethren, be srong in the Lord, and in the power of his might. Put on the whole armour of God, that ye may be able to stand against the wiles of the devil (Ephesians 6:10–11).

We have been looking, during several studies, at the various aspects of this great truth, the whole truth of the Bible, and have been trying to discover how it is used by the Holy Spirit to produce our sanctification. I do not claim that we have dealt with it in an exhaustive manner, we obviously have not, but I have been trying to take out and to select the greater, larger and more obvious principles. We come, now, to an essential aspect of this question of our sanctification through the truth, for no consideration of this doctrine would be adequate without including the teaching which we find stated so perfectly in Ephesians 6, starting especially at verse 10: 'Finally, my brethren, be strong in the Lord, and in the power of his might. Put on the whole armour of God, that ye may be able to stand against the wiles of the devil.'

Now we have seen that God has many ways of promoting our sanctification, which are all taught and enumerated in the word. We saw very clearly at one point that God can use circumstances, that at times he chastises us through them, all with the desire and object of increasing our sanctification. In exactly the same way, it is perfectly clear from the teaching of the Scriptures that God uses even the activity of the devil and his powers to promote our sanctification, which is why we must of necessity look at it. Here is the teaching, which is so plain and clear, that we 'wrestle not [only or merely] against flesh and blood, but against principalities, against powers, against the rulers of the darkness of this world, against spiritual wickedness in high places [in the heavenlies]' (v. 12).

But before we come to analyse this in detail, I feel constrained to ask why it is that this aspect of the truth is so little stressed in our day and generation? It is one of those aspects of truth that is neglected and almost forgotten. Furthermore, I am not here referring to those who are outside the church, nor to those who hold so-called liberal views of the Bible and its teaching, I am referring to those who regard themselves as evangelical Christians. Why is it that we have neglected this? I am constrained to ask that question because you cannot read the Bible without finding teaching about the devil everywhere. Indeed, I would not hesitate to go so far as to say that without this, one cannot understand the Bible at all. It is no use just saying that you believe in sanctification and in a positive act of salvation. We need to know what we are to be delivered *from* and we do not begin to understand that until we really see and grasp this aspect of the teaching. The Bible is not only an outline of the way of salvation; it contains the only teaching that we have concerning the cause of our fall and of our trouble. The Bible shows us that the activity of the devil and his hosts is the whole cause of man's troubles: and yet we so frequently neglect this teaching. When we look at the world in the light of this teaching we see that the activity of the devil is a major factor in the whole life of mankind.

But, to put the argument at its strongest, is it not something we see so clearly in the earthly life of our Lord himself? Our Lord, while he was here in this world, was struggling and fighting against these powers. The biblical view of life in this world is that it is a mighty, spiritual conflict, and even the Son of God himself when he was here in the flesh was involved in this. We all think of his temptation in the wilderness, and we are reminded also of how the devil came back to him in the Garden of Gethsemane and upon the cross itself. There was a mighty battle going on, a tremendous spiritual conflict. We can feel the tension as we read the accounts. Then, when we come to the lives of the apostles, we find exactly the same thing. The apostle Paul always gives the impression that he knew something about this battle against these powers and forces. We wrestle and struggle against them, he says, for this is the thing with which we are confronted: we are not merely up against man but infinitely more important are these tremendous spiritual powers that are arrayed against us.

In other words, it does seem to me that we cannot really read our New Testament without being conscious of this spiritual tension, this spiritual conflict, that is going on. That is why these men prayed so much, and, perhaps, we pray so little, because somehow or other we have forgotten this spiritual conflict in the midst of which our whole life is set. Indeed, when you read the history of God's people throughout the centuries you will find that they testify to the same thing. We all remember the famous story of Martin Luther. One afternoon in his study he was so conscious of the presence of the devil that he took hold of his inkpot and hurled it at him. I do not think that that speaks to us modern Christians as it should. Are we aware of that? Do we know anything about that when we tend to dismiss Luther as almost being a psychopath? Is it imagination? But it is the testimony of all God's people, especially those who have been concerned about knowing God most intimately, those who have striven after holiness, those who have worked out their salvation with fear and trembling. They all testify to the same thing, to this trouble in the spiritual realm, this conflict, this battle.

So, therefore, we must of necessity face the question as to why we so seldom hear about this, and why it is preached about so infrequently. Why, too, do we speak about it so infrequently in conversation with Christian people and as we give our testimonies to one another? I have little hesitation in answering that question. I feel that the main explanation is a false doctrine of sanctification which makes sanctification appear quite simple and easy. We think that we have only one thing to do, then all will be well, and we will live this easy life ever afterwards. But the result is that we hear nothing about this wrestling 'not against flesh and blood, but against principalities, against powers'. We have been taught a doctrine which gives the impression that any sense of tension or struggle in any respect is wrong and false; that we all ought to be always at ease and perfectly happy. Of course, we all understand the desire to be happy, but whether we should desire ease is another matter. However, the point I am making is that surely that view of sanctification inevitably conflicts with this particular aspect of the truth that we are considering together here.

Furthermore, has it not happened because we have been concentrating upon only one aspect of sanctification and not upon the whole? We have been so concerned about a particular sin which tends to get us down that we have forgotten the principalities and powers. Consequently, we have regarded sanctification as something that gives us deliverance from one particular sin, as a kind of clinic to which we go to be delivered from that sin. We have been so constantly dwelling on that one aspect of sanctification and of the truth, that we have failed to remember these other aspects. We have forgotten the devil, the fight and the conflict, and have thereby tended to forget that we need the whole of the truth before our sanctification can be truly promoted. I do feel, therefore, that this is a vitally important matter. We often hear people talking about the 'lost note' in modern evangelism, and for myself I have no doubt that *this* is the note which has been lost. As a result, we have somehow or other lost this conception of the bigness and the mightiness of this Christian life, the fact that we are engaged in a struggle between the almighty God and this amazing power that is set against him, and that if we are truly Christian we, too, are partakers in the struggle.

So let us look at this. Obviously I cannot in one study hope to deal with it in the way it deserves. I am simply giving you some headings in order to show the big principles. So let us, first of all, look at the struggle. This is, we are told, the conflict 'against principalities, against powers, against the rulers of the darkness of this world, against spiritual wickedness in high places.' We shall not go into detail about the words, because what matters is that we should have some understanding of what they represent. We are concerned about the devil; you know the names that are given to him – Satan, Beelzebub, the prince of the power of the air, the god of this world, the prince of this world, and so on.

And what do these names tell us? Once again, the first thing we must bear in mind is that the devil is a person. I have already emphasised the truth that the Holy Spirit is a Person because we tend to forget that and think of him as an influence; and it is exactly the same with the devil. We tend so much to think of the devil as just some general influence, or perhaps not even that, we merely explain his activity in psychological terms. But according to the Scriptures there is a person called the devil who is the 'god of this world', and the Bible teaches, too, that he was a very high, bright and powerful angelic being, created by God before the world was ever made, before man ever came into existence. But he raised himself against God and rebelled against him. He pitted himself against God. The implication is that it was his ambition, his desire, to be equal with God; he refused to subordinate himself to God or to acknowledge God as supreme. So he rebelled against God and persuaded other angels to agree with him, and there was this mighty fall in the angelic realm.

There is, therefore, a kingdom of Satan, a kingdom of the devil. He is the head of that kingdom and he has power and he has his emissaries. That is what is meant by 'principalities, powers and the rulers of the darkness of this world, the spiritual wickedness in high places.' I shall not go into a detailed consideration of what 'high places' or 'heavenlies' mean; it does not matter as long as we know that there is a kingdom with all these forces and powers, of which the devil is the head, and that his ambition is to destroy the work of God; that he pits himself against the almighty God and all who belong to him, and that he is intent upon the destruction of all that God is and all that God has done.

The next thing that is emphasised is the greatness of the struggle, which is due very largely to the greatness of the devil's power. That is why our neglect of the devil is so serious. It is also why the tendency of Christian people to laugh at the mention of the name of the devil is not only alarming, but is a manifestation of the grossest ignorance. The devil is not a joke. He is, according to the Scriptures, such a mighty power that he did not hesitate to pit himself against the Son of God and even appeared at one point to have triumphed. What is this greatness? Well, he is described as 'a roaring lion ... seeking whom he may devour' (1 Pet 5:8) – that is the devil. Our Lord himself referred to him as 'the strong man armed' whose 'goods are at peace' (Lk 11:22) – such is his power. He is altogether more powerful than man, more powerful than man even in a state of perfection, because he was too much for Adam and Eve. It was he who persuaded, and apparently with great ease, this man in a state of perfection. Indeed, he is even greater in power than the archangel Michael himself, because we read in the epistle of Jude that even the archangel 'durst not bring against him a railing accusation, but said, The Lord rebuke thee' (v. 9).

That is something of the power that is opposed to us; such is the struggle in which we are involved. The moment we belong to God and his Christ we are engaged in this struggle. Before that, we belonged to the kingdom of darkness – we were part of the goods he keeps at peace. We also see something of his power as we read the book of Job. He is one who is able to wander to and fro in the earth (Job 1:7). In Job chapter 1 he has power even over the winds and the very elements. In Hebrews he is described as the one who 'had the power of death' (Heb 2:14). I am saying all these things so that we may have some conception of his power. Paul describes him in Ephesians 2:2 as 'the prince of the power of the air, the spirit that now worketh in the children of disobedience'. Then in 2 Corinthians 4:4 the Apostle does not hesitate to say that if men and women do not believe the gospel of the glorious God, there is only one reason for it, it is that their minds have been blinded by 'the god of this world'.

Such, then, is something of this terrible power of the devil and his emissaries and forces. He is set against God and his work, and God's people and all that they have, and he is intent upon our destruction. He will do anything he can to hinder our sanctification, to bring us again out of the kingdom of God, and back into his own kingdom. That is what he is concerned about, and he rules in the world, and in the flesh, attacking us from the outside in this violent manner. Nothing is so important, therefore, as that we should know something of his power and of his methods, and that is the thing that Paul is concerned about here in Ephesians 6.

And then, in addition to his strength, we must also emphasise his subtlety. The Apostle speaks of the 'wiles of the devil'. I wonder if you have ever stopped to think about them? Paul writes in 2 Corinthians 2:11: 'We are not ignorant of his devices.' I am afraid that one of our greatest troubles is that we *are* ignorant of them. We do not seem to know enough about his subtlety, which is why he so often fools us. Consider these statements: 'As the serpent,' says Paul again, 'beguiled Eve' (2 Cor 11:3) – read Genesis 3 and watch him doing it. He comes as a friend, as one who is interested in us, someone whose supreme concern is our well-being and our success. In short, he *beguiles* us. Why, says Paul, he can transform himself into an angel of light (2 Cor 11:14). He can come, as it were, as an advocate of the gospel, as one who is interested in evangelism. He proposes methods to us that are so much better than the biblical ones!

So if he can do all that, it is not surprising that we may be ignorant of his devices; that is why in 2 Corinthians 2 Paul is emphasising the kind of conflict in which we are engaged. The devil is not someone who comes in an openly evil manner, as someone who is obviously opposed to God. No, rather, he came to our Lord in this way: If you are the Son of God, why do you not feed yourself? If you are the Son of God, why do you not rely on his promises and cast yourself down from this pinnacle and give the glory to the greatness of God? You say you are interested in the kingdoms of this world, I will give you all that if you will bow down and worship me. The devil seems to be concerned about the evangelism of God's kingdom – he comes as an angel of light. So are we aware of his wiles? Are we on guard? Are we watching? That is the exhortation of the Scriptures: 'Watch ye, stand fast in the faith' (1 Cor 16:13). You must watch and pray. We find these exhortations everywhere, because of this spiritual conflict, and yet how infrequently we talk about it, how infrequently we look out for it in our daily lives and in our spiritual activities. The subtlety of it all!

But let us go a step further, let us be more practical and come down to details. In what ways does he manifest this power and this subtlety? This is a great theme, even though at this point we shall only be dealing with it briefly. Here we come to this whole realm where so many seem to find it difficult to differentiate between the psychological, the physical and the spiritual; but let us confine ourselves to the answer to that question given by Paul in Ephesians 6. The only way to deal with him is to put on the whole armour of God. Paul is not content with stating that in general, so he divides it into its component parts in order that we may follow the lines along which the devil comes. There he is opposed to us in all his subtlety and his malignity. He throws these darts at us, these fiery arrows which, when they strike an object, burst into flame.

What are these innuendoes, these things that he is throwing at us as God's people? Well, here are some of them. Firstly, there are doubts – I mean by that, doubts about the faith, about the gospel, uncertainty about it with respect to ourselves, doubts as to whether we are saved. Now I know that large numbers of Christian people today testify that ever since they were converted they have never been tempted to doubt. I wonder whether that fits into this passage? If you read the lives of some of the greatest saints you will find that the devil has tried to persuade them to doubt not only their own salvation, but the gospel itself. We must be careful and examine once more the type of belief and teaching which seems to exclude doubts entirely. In view of the adversary by whom we are confronted does it not savour rather of the psychological than of the spiritual? He insinuates the doubts; it is he who throws the fiery darts.

And then there are all the types and kinds of fear, not only about our own salvation or a wrong fear of God and a fear of death, but sometimes a fear of the physical aspect of death. Then perhaps one of his favourite methods is to produce a state of introspection and morbidity. We all know what is meant by introspection – it is self-examination carried out to a point at which it ceases to be beneficial, so that instead of examining yourself in a spiritual way to see whether you are in the faith or not and looking to Christ, you spend the whole of your time looking into yourself, examining the blackness of your own heart. You become such an expert in your own deficiencies, in the blackness of your own condition and the blackness of your own soul, that you drop down into the depths. That is no longer self-examination, but introspection, and it leads, of course, to this state of morbidity in which you are so aware of your own unworthiness and sinfulness that it becomes a cloud which hides the face of your Saviour. It almost seems to do away with Calvary and you are persuaded that nothing can save you. You are so aware of your sin and your blackness that you tend to allow yourself to see nothing else and it obscures the gospel.

How often we prove, by our conduct and behaviour, the truth of the Bible; we always oscillate between extremes. One is the condition in which we never examine ourselves at all. We say we must always look at Christ and not at ourselves; but the Scripture tells us to look at ourselves. We are so objective and we have forgotten the devil. We are not aware of the spiritual conflict at all, we are perfectly happy all the day long and nothing whatsoever troubles us. Then we go right from that to the other extreme, in which we are down in the depths of introspection and morbidity, which is also always produced by the devil. The devil as an angel of light comes and says, 'The Scriptures tell you to examine yourself, so you must do so.' Then he starts us on the process which we have just seen and he does it to such a degree that the end of it is spiritual depression of which there is a great deal in these days. (I do not think, however, that there is as much as there once was, and I am even prepared to say that

that is a bad thing. I prefer spiritual depression to that superficial glibness which is not even aware of the process, but both are wrong.) It is not that he has made you cease to be a Christian; but he has made you a miserable one, and because of that you are a bad recommendation to the gospel. He fills you with such a concern about yourself that you have no time to think about anybody else. You cannot forget yourself, you are always down in the depths, and it is all the work of these principalities and powers. It is a part of the method of the devil as an angel of light.

But he does not even stop at that. How many of God's greatest saints have testified to the fact that they have been attacked by blasphemous thoughts entering their minds? Where have they come from? They are fiery darts thrown by the devil. Do you know anything about these? Have you been on your knees praying to God, and then found that the most horrible blasphemous thoughts have come to you? They have come from the devil. He not only hurls doubts, he even puts these vile, awful thoughts into your mind. Then there are temptations – he is the merest tyro in this matter who thinks he has once and for all finished with certain temptations; because they may come back to you at any moment, the devil will see to that. And we must realise here the importance of differentiating between temptation and sin. To be tempted does not mean you have committed an act of sin. The devil can subject the greatest saint to some of the grossest temptations to sin even after years of growth in the Christian life. It is the devil who does it, not the man himself. The devil hurls it at him – it is, once more, the fiery darts of the wicked one.

And on top of it all – and I must mention it because it is to be stressed in this passage – what does the Apostle mean in Ephesians 6:13 by 'the evil day'? I think he means that over and above all these things we have been looking at, there are special occasions when the devil seems to be let loose and comes upon us in all the might of his ferocity. Job knew something about that. But let me put it to you in the words of a great hymn written in the eighteenth century by the saintly

John Newton – he says it all perfectly. I do not know that it is in a single modern hymnary belonging to any denomination – such are the times in which we live – and to find it we must go to the Gadsby Hymnbook!

> I asked the Lord that I might grow
> In faith and love and every grace
> Might more of His salvation know
> And seek more earnestly His face,
> 'Twas He who taught me thus to pray,
> And He, I trust, has answered prayer,
> But it has been in such a way,
> As almost drove me to despair.
> I hoped that in some favor'd hour,
> At once He'd answer my request,
> And by His love's constraining power
> Subdue my sins and give me rest.
> Instead of this, He made me feel
> The hidden evils of my heart,
> And let the angry powers of hell
> Assault my soul in every part.
> Yea more, with His own hand He seem'd
> Intent to aggravate my woe
> Cross'd all the fair designs I schemed,
> Blasted my gourd and laid me low.
> Lord, why is this, I trembling cried,
> Wilt Thou pursue Thy worm to death?
> It is in this way, the Lord replied,
> I answer prayer for grace and faith,
> These inward trials I employ,
> From self and pride to set thee free;
> And brake thy schemes of earthly joy,
> That thou may'st seek thy all in Me.

You see what he is saying? John Newton, having been converted from the terrible life he once lived, was now concerned about his sanctification, and he prayed to God that in one stroke he would cleanse his heart and deliver him from all sin, that he might enjoy peace and rest for ever afterwards. He asked the

Lord to sanctify him, but what in fact happened to him was that he was given a view of himself and of the blackness and foulness of his own heart. Then hell was let loose upon him and he could not understand it. So he asked God why he was doing it, and that was the answer – God said that that was his way of sanctifying people. You have to have self crushed out and it is the only way. The 'positive' gospel will not do it and so you have to have hell let loose and you will be crushed to the ground. You will cry to me, says God, and then I will tell you that I have to smash you before I can reveal myself to you. Yes, God sometimes allows the devil to do as he did in the cases of Job and John Newton. Do you know anything of that sort of experience? If you read the lives of the greatest saints, you will find they all knew something about it. They never knew short cuts to sanctification, but they knew something about this. This is God's way. Thus it is clear that God permits this and uses it to produce and promote our sanctification.

Lastly, how do we meet the struggle? How do we stand in such a condition? The answer is given perfectly here in Ephesians. The first thing is to realise that this is so, that this has happened. For if we do not realise that we are involved in this spiritual struggle, it means that we are so duped by Satan that we have not been aware that he is there. We know nothing about him as an angel of light. The second thing, obviously, is that the moment we realise this, we know at once that there is only one strength that is great enough to stand up to this, and that is the strength of the Lord: 'Finally, my brethren, be strong in the Lord and in the power of his might' (v. 10). Nothing else can do it, for the devil is stronger even than the archangel, and who are we?

Therefore we must put on the whole armour of God, and the apostle Paul takes us through the parts. The first is truth. This means that the only way finally to stand in this day is to know the truth, the faith, to have a clear knowledge and understanding of the gospel – and that is why I have been going through it all in these studies. It is only as we have this whole armour that we stand – the whole gospel – sanctification is not one special doctrine, it is the whole doctrine, the holiness of God all the way through everything else. There must be no doubt or uncertainty as to the way of righteousness. We must rely entirely upon the finished work of Christ – justification by faith only. We must be absolutely clear about it because if we are not, the devil will get us. We must realise our utter dependence thus upon God and have a clear knowledge of the fact that we are no longer under the dominion of the devil. We must read Romans 6, we must study it and realise that though the devil attacks us, we are not under his dominion any longer, and how vital this is!

'That wicked one,' says John in 1 John 5:18, 'toucheth him not,' but though he cannot touch us, he can frighten us, he can throw his darts at us. But he will never get us back into his kingdom again; we have been taken out of it and are now under the dominion of the Son of God. Let us make certain of it, so that even when the devil attacks us, we can defy him to the face and say, 'You cannot touch me!' Though he is our adversary, though he comes as a roaring lion, we are to resist him and stand steadfast in the faith. So we must know the faith. If we neglect Christian doctrine, it just means that we are ignorant of the devil. For, ultimately, the way to defeat him and to master and defy him, is to stand in the doctrine, not a superficial Bible study but the great biblical doctrines. The more we know of them, the more we will be able to withstand the devil.

And then, in addition to all that, we need to be 'shod with the preparation of the gospel of peace'. In other words, we need to be quick, we need to be subtle ourselves, because he is subtle. We must answer him and tell him that we can work as quickly as he can. It is a battle of wits. So have these sandals on your feet, says Paul, in order that you can move as quickly as he can. And the gospel enables us to do this. But even after all this is done, we need to remain on the offensive, we must, 'take … the sword of the Spirit, which is the word of God' and strike at the devil with the word. We must attack him, and when he comes we must strike him – that is the method. There is the essence of it, and we must work it out in detail. Then in verse 18 Paul adds 'watching with all perseverance and supplication for all saints' –

we must always be watching and praying. Watch, stand fast in the faith, quit yourselves like men, be strong: that is it; the same truth is repeated everywhere – watchfulness, waiting for the subtlety. We must learn to discriminate, we must not believe in everything that appears to be good; everything that appears good is not of necessity of God. The devil is subtle, we must differentiate, we must be watchful and we are ever exhorted to do this.

Above all, Paul exhorts us to prayerfulness: living and dwelling in God's presence, drinking in his life and being constantly built up in the faith. And so, in this way, in spite of the power and the malignity and the subtlety of the devil, we shall be able to stand; and even should an evil day come, when hell itself is let loose upon us, though we may not understand, we shall be able to stand in his might and in the power of his love, we shall overcome the enemy. O may the Lord God open our eyes to realise this aspect of our Christian life and warfare, because it is only as we realise something about it that our sanctification will proceed gloriously and we shall see that in every way God himself is sanctifying us.

11

The Unity of the Spirit

Neither pray I for these alone, but for them also which shall believe on me through their word; that they all may be one; as thou, Father, art in me, and I in thee, that they also may be one in us: that the world may believe that thou hast sent me. And the glory which thou gavest me I have given them; that they may be one, even as we are one: I in them, and thou in me, that they may be made perfect in one; and that the world may know that thou hast sent me, and hast loved them, as thou hast loved me (John 17:20–23).

We come now to deal with a petition which our Lord has already offered on behalf of his disciples as it is recorded in the eleventh verse of this chapter: 'And now I am no more in the world, but these are in the world, and I come to thee. Holy Father, keep through thine own name those whom thou hast given me, that they may be one, as we are.' In our analysis of this chapter[1] we have pointed out that it can be divided into three main sections: the first from verses 1 to 5, in which our Lord prays for himself; the second from verses 6 to 19, where he prays particularly and more especially for his immediate followers, the disciples that are around and about him; and then the third from verse 20 to the end, where he prays not only for them but for all who throughout the centuries, until the end of time, shall believe on him.

---

[1] See Volume 1, *Saved in Eternity* (Kingsway Publications 1988).

We spent most of our time on that section which runs from verses 6 to 19, and we showed that our Lord gives certain reasons why he prays for his disciples. We then went on to study the petitions that he offered on their behalf. There were three main petitions. The first was that they might be kept from the evil one, from the evil that is in the world, but supremely from the evil one himself: our Lord is going to heaven and he is leaving them in an antagonistic world, and they are opposed by this powerful, subtle enemy, so he prays his Father to keep them from the evil one. Then, as a continuation of that petition, he prays the petition which we have been considering very fully for several chapters: 'Sanctify them through thy truth, thy word is truth.' The way to be kept from the evil one is, of course, to be sanctified; it is God alone who sanctifies, and he does it through the truth, in the way that we have seen.

So now we come to the third and last of these petitions, and it is in this petition that our Lord prays that his people and his followers might be one, even as he and his Father are one. And what we really have in verses 20–23 is an elaboration of that particular petition. He talks to them, as it were, about that petition which he has already offered, and now he repeats it, and repeats it more than once. He elaborates his reasons for doing so, and explains what he means by it. Clearly we are face to face here with a very important principle in connection with our Christian life, and it is essential that we should consider it.

It is a principle which is of particular interest at this present hour, because I suppose that if there is one thing that characterises the life of the church and of Christian people more than anything else in this particular generation, it is the interest in what is called 'ecumenicity'. We are constantly reading about it and conferences and meetings are being held almost without intermission, with respect to it. An interest in it began about 1910, but it has been particularly to the forefront during the last twenty years. What we are generally told can be summarised like this: the greatest scandal in the world is a disunited church, and this scandal must be removed; it must also be removed because it is the greatest hindrance to evangelism. It is the multiplicity of denominations that constitutes one of the greatest hindrances to men and women who are outside the church believing the gospel. If we could only get rid of these denominations and have one great world, or 'super', church, then people would be ready to listen to the gospel and probably to accept it. Further, this movement for church unity – this movement of ecumenicity – is 'the greatest movement and manifestation of the Holy Spirit since the Day of Pentecost'. That is a summary of what many people are saying.

In the light of all this, we obviously must give some consideration to this subject. But our method of doing so is rather different from that which, speaking generally, characterises the life of the church at the present time; for you notice at once, that there are certain things that are characteristic of all this modern interest and talk about ecumenicity. The people concerned are very fond of quoting John 17, it seems to be *the* chapter on which they base everything, but what interests me is that they invariably seem to speak of this chapter as if there were nothing in it at all except this plea for unity. Well, I think that the time we have spent with this chapter is proof positive that that, at any rate, is completely wrong! There is no richer chapter in the whole Bible than John 17 and we have done some thirteen studies on the first five verses only.[1]

How little we hear about the work which the Father had given the Son to do, about the people whom he had given to him, and so on. Instead, the impression is given that John 17 has only one message in it, and that is this great question of unity.

In other words, we see the terrible danger of isolating a text, extracting it from its context, and forgetting the need to have a balanced view of Scripture and to grasp what we may call the wholeness and the unity of the scriptural teaching. Because if you read this chapter thoroughly, and study it as it should be studied, you will see that this whole question of unity is not something that our Lord deals with on its own; it is a part of the entire outlook, and of this whole petition that he offers for his

---

[1] Volume 1, *Saved in Eternity* (Kingsway Publications 1988).

followers. It is not a doctrine that is to be found in isolation. And we have said the same thing about the doctrine of sanctification also. For that is our trouble; we constantly regard the truth of God as if it were a number of propositions, instead of realising the truth as a whole, seeing that each particular part belongs to the whole, and that if it is to be grasped truly, and in proportion, it must be taken in its context. We must arrive at our particular point only after we have followed the scriptural method, and the scriptural pattern.

My suggestion, then, as we approach this subject of unity, is that we can only begin to understand it if we are perfectly clear in our minds as to what constitutes a Christian. Our Lord says that in verses 6 to 8 of this chapter, and we spent some time considering the subject. The modern idea seems to be that it does not matter about the definition; if people call themselves Christians, that is all that matters. But our Lord takes care to define who a Christian is, and to show how Christians are utterly different from the world. In the same way, he has also dealt with this vital subject of our sanctification. I cannot see, as I study this chapter, that one can ever say that it does not matter very much what people believe, or how they live or behave, so long as they call themselves Christians. According to our Lord, we use this designation of a Christian wrongly. Christians are those who have been sanctified by the Father – and nobody else – and you see the relevance of this in the modern situation. Surely we must all agree that not all who use the name Christian can, in the light of this chapter, be called Christians; it is not that we sit in judgement on others, but we do face the word of God and seek to be guided by it.

So it seems to me that the most convenient thing to do is to extract the principles which are clearly indicated here by what our Lord says. The first is that we must be clear as to the nature of this unity about which he is speaking. You notice that every time he mentions it, he does so in a particular way: 'Holy Father, keep through thine own name those whom thou hast given me, that they may be one, as we are' (v. 11). Then he goes on in verse 20: 'Neither pray I for these alone, but for them also which shall believe on me through their word; that they all may be one; as thou, Father, art in me, and I in thee, that they also may be one in us; that the world may believe that thou hast sent me' – and again he repeats it – 'And the glory which thou gavest me I have given them; that they may be one, even as we are one.' And then he is not content even with that: 'I in them, and thou in me, that they may be made perfect in one; and that the world may know that thou hast sent me, and hast loved them, as thou hast loved me.'

It is to me almost incomprehensible that people can quote this seventeenth chapter of John on unity, while at the same time they seem to forget and ignore entirely what our Lord is always so careful to repeat and elaborate every time he mentions the subject of unity. Such people are thinking in terms of external unity, a mechanical, organisational unity, while all the time our Lord is teaching what we must describe as an inner and mystical unity. The unity that he is concerned about is the unity of life and the unity of spirit. He makes that very plain by the analogy he draws between Christian unity and the unity in the Godhead, an analogy which he is always careful to keep in the forefront. In other words, if we are to understand the character of this unity about which our Lord is concerned, we must realise that there are certain indications of mystical unity which are very clearly given in the Scriptures. Now let me say at once that this is a very high and difficult subject. I believe that, in the last analysis, it is the most abstruse subject in the entire realm of revelation, because we are, of necessity, considering the Almighty God himself. But our Lord compels us to do this, because he always considers the unity which is to characterise his people as being analogous to this other mystical, eternal unity.

Four types of unity are dealt with in the Scriptures. The first is the unity between the three Persons of the blessed Holy Trinity – 'I in them, and thou in me'; 'My Father and I are One' – that inscrutable eternal unity which exists and subsists between them. Of course, let me repeat, we are dealing with something that patently is entirely beyond human understanding. We say,

'How can three be one and one be three at the same time?' And the answer is that we cannot understand it. The Scripture tells us that the blessed God is three Persons, and yet that the three are one, one eternal substance, three Persons and yet not three Gods but one God. There is only one true and living God, but that one eternal God exists as three separate and distinct Persons, and yet there is this perfect, marvellous, wonderful, mystic unity. That is the kind of unity about which our Lord is speaking.

The second kind of unity of which we read in the Bible is the union of the two natures in the one Person of the Lord Jesus Christ, and that is the great theme of the New Testament. Here is the Lord Jesus Christ, perfect God, perfect Man, truly God, truly Man, and yet he is not two Persons. It is rank heresy to think of him as such because he is one Person, but in that one Person there are these two natures, not at all mixed, not at all fused or intermingled: they are there, but they are quite distinct. Yet they are not separate, because there is a unity between them, and it is a perfect union, the mystical unity of the two natures in the one Person of the Lord Jesus Christ. That is another mystical unity and it is analogous, obviously, to the union that exists between the three Persons of the blessed Holy Trinity.

Now the next unity that our Lord speaks of is the union of his people with himself. He deals with that at great length in chapters 14 to 16 of John's Gospel, but we find it in many other places also, and the apostles deal with it in their epistles: 'Christ in you, the hope of glory' (Col 1:27); 'I live; yet not I, but Christ liveth in me' (Gal 2:20). There it is in particular, but the whole body of Christian people is in Christ. We read in Ephesians 4, about the wonderful body, Christ being the head, and we all members of the body; it is the mystical union which is between Christ and the church which Paul expresses in Ephesians 5 in terms of the illustration of the union between the bridegroom and the bride.

And the last, of course, is the one with which we are dealing here; the union of Christian people among themselves and with one another, and the point I would emphasise is that our Lord always, everywhere, teaches that this is to be thought of in terms analogous to the others which I have already mentioned. When we come to this, we must not forget the others; we must not suddenly become external, mechanical or organisational in our ideas and concepts. The unity which he prays for, for his people, is the unity which is analogous to that of the Father, the Son and the Holy Spirit – this mystical union between the blessed Persons – and to the unity between Christ and the church. Now this can never be emphasised too frequently. It is a spiritual unity, 'the unity of the Spirit', as Paul puts it in Ephesians 4:3, and the same thing that he elaborates in 1 Corinthians 12.

It is the only unity that the New Testament knows, and it is the only unity in which it is at all interested. So we must get right out of the realm of the mechanical and external and organisational, and we must say that whatever this unity is, it is similar to that wonderful union which is between Christ and his followers: '... that they all may be one; as thou, Father, art in me, and I in thee, that they also may be one in us' (v. 21). Then he elaborates it again: 'even as we are one: I in them, and thou in me, that they may be made perfect in one' (vv. 22, 23). There is no gap, there is to be no interval, it is all in a series, and that is the nature of the unity about which he is concerned. The only other point I should like to make about the character of this unity is that our Lord is not praying anywhere in this chapter that this union may come to be; what he prays here is that this union, that is already in existence, may be kept, may be continued, and may be preserved by his Father.

That, then, is the nature of the unity, so we now move on to our second point: what are the conditions of this union? What is it that makes and produces it? Those are vital questions, especially in the light of the modern discussion on unity, and the answer given here is perfectly clear. It is in the twentieth verse: 'Neither pray I for these alone, but for them also which shall believe on me through their word.' What, then, is going to preserve this unity? 'Well,' says our Lord in effect, 'it is the word, which these followers of mine are going to preach after I am gone; and as the result of the preaching of this word people are going to be converted and come into the church.' In verses 16 and 17 he says that it is like this: 'They are not of the world, even as I am not of the world. Sanctify them through thy truth, thy word is truth.' And then he prays not for them alone, but also for all others, 'who shall believe on me through their word'. The same thing, of course, has already been said in verse 11, and we saw, when we considered in detail our Lord's phrase 'through thine own name', that it meant that the Lord Jesus Christ has revealed his Father's name to those people who belong to him, but not to the world.[1] The world does not understand it, but these people do, and what makes us really the people of God is that through the word we have understood the meaning of the name of the Lord.

So we arc back again to this same question of the word; indeed, we might argue that the one thing that produces unity is what our Lord tells them in verses 6 to 9: 'I have manifested thy name unto the men which thou gavest me out of the world: thine they were, and thou gavest them me; and they have kept thy word. Now they have known that all things whatsoever thou hast given me are of thee. For I have given unto them the words which thou gavest me; and they have received them, and have known surely that I came out from thee, and they have believed that thou didst send me. I pray for them: I pray not for the world, but for them which thou hast given me, for they are thine.' That is the character of these people: 'I pray for them, I pray not for the world ...' the world does not believe these things.

Now surely this ought to be abundantly clear to us. What makes these people, and what makes the greatest unity of these people, is this word, this message of God which has been given to them, first by the Lord himself, and subsequently by his apostles and disciples – that is the basis of the unity. We can translate that into modern terms and put it like this: what makes the greatest unity is the common faith, what we believe, what

---

[1] See Volume 2, *Safe in the World* (Kingsway Publications 1988).

we have received together, and what nobody else has received. That is the unity which our Lord is concerned about in this chapter; it is all entirely dependent upon this particular word, and it is only as men and women are agreed about this word and accept it and subscribe to the same faith and to the same common salvation, that there can be any conceivable unity among them; any other unity is of no value whatsoever.

But he also puts that in a slightly different form. The word, after all, creates the unity by bringing us into a particular relationship to him – that is the message of verse 22: 'And the glory which thou gavest me I have given them; that they may be one, even as we are one.' He says that it is because he has given them this glory that they are one, even as he and the Father are one. He speaks also of this glory which the Father has given to him: 'The glory which thou gavest me I have given them.' What, then, is this glory? Obviously it cannot be the eternal glory of the Son of God, because that is not a glory which has been given him by the Father, it is a glory which he has always shared with the Father from all eternity. It must, therefore, be some kind of glory that the Father gave to the Son while he was here in this life and in this world, and a glory which, in turn, he is able to impart unto his own followers. And what is that? I suggest to you that there is only one adequate answer to that question, and that is this special relationship to God which becomes ours through the work and the operation of the Holy Spirit. While our Lord was here in this world and when he had taken upon himself human nature, when he had decided to live life in this world as a man and in the likeness of sinful flesh, the Father gave him this glory, this union with himself, this intimate relationship, this knowledge of the Father, so that he would always depend upon his Father and be always receiving grace and glory from him. And that is what, he here tells us, he has also given to his followers.

If you want that in detail, go back to chapters 14 to 16 and read there his teaching about the work and the operation of the Holy Spirit. He is going to send them the Spirit, and the effect of that will be that he will dwell in them. They will be in him, he will be in them, and they will not feel that they are orphans because they will have an intimacy with him such as they have never had before; that is the glory which he gives. It is, in other words, as I have shown earlier, our being united to him and his being in us – we in him and he in us – and thus we are able to receive of his grace and of his glory, and grace for grace. Now what I am emphasising is that all this is obviously impossible apart from the word. It is the word that teaches this, it is the word that mediates this to us, so that all who really are to receive this, receive it through and by means of the word, and that, I suggest to you, is the only union and unity which is dealt with in this chapter, the only unity in which our Lord is interested.

Let me put it like this: a mere coalition of organisations or denominations has in reality nothing whatsoever to do with this unity. Indeed, it may even be a danger. The unity that our Lord is concerned about is a unity which is spiritual. It consists of a unity of spirits, and it is a unity, therefore, which is based solidly upon the truth. It is based upon the whole doctrine – regeneration and the rebirth, the receiving of the Holy Spirit – and obviously the doctrine must be dependent ultimately upon the Person of our Lord and upon his work. It is a unity of people who have become spiritual and who have been born again: we are made one with one another, because we first of all are united to Christ and made one with him, and, through him, one with God.

Therefore, to argue that the one thing that matters is some sort of organisational or external unity is not only to fall short of this conception, it is even to do something which is highly dangerous. If a man comes to me and says, 'It does not matter what you believe as long as you call yourself a Christian,' I reply, 'No, that is impossible.' And I must ask that man certain questions and get his answers. What is his view of the Lord Jesus Christ? Is the Lord Jesus Christ just a man to him? There are many people in this world who call themselves Christians, yet who, alas, regard the Lord Jesus Christ as nothing but a man. Well, all I can say to that is that I have no fellowship with such people. I have no unity with them for they take from the very foundation and basis of my faith, and my whole position and standing. What do these people believe about the work of the Lord Jesus Christ? What is their view of his death? Is it just a tragedy; is it just the death of a passive resister; is it the death of someone who was not understood by his contemporaries? Is it a murderous death or is it a substitutionary death? Is it the Son of God dying because that is the only way whereby my sins may be forgiven, and therefore the essential preliminary to my becoming a child of God, and a partaker of the divine nature? If it is essential, and the other man says it is not, how can it be possible for there to be unity between us? And the same is true with all these other cardinal doctrines of the Christian faith.

Now there is no unity unless we stand on this – one Lord, one faith, one baptism. There is only one Lord Jesus Christ, and I must be clear about his Person and about his work. There is only one faith (I do not mean here my faith in him, but the faith about him), the faith that the apostles preached. They preached that Jesus is the Lord, the Son of God, that he died for our sins and that he was made a substitute for us. That is their faith, the word that they preached, and it was as the result of hearing and believing this word that the people became members of the church, and one with others who were in the church before them.

So you see that these things are vital; this is the unity that was to be found in the early church; it is the unity that is found at all times of true reformation and revival; and, thank God, it is the unity that is in existence at the present time, in spite of the multiplicity of denominations and organisations. There is nothing, I sometimes think, in the realm of Christian life and experience, which is quite as wonderful as the demonstration of this unity. Is it not a fact, my friends, that we who are Christians recognise one another the moment we meet? It is the greatest privilege in my life as the minister of a church that as I stand in the vestry to meet the people coming in to see me, often people whom I have never seen in my life before, that I at once recognise them. I know them. I know that they are brothers and sisters of mine. I do not know where they come from – they come from all parts of the world – and yet at once I know them, and I feel that I have known them for years. Why? Because it is the unity of the Spirit.

I can go even further – and let me put it quite simply and bluntly – I have some interesting experiences in that room in this very connection. Some people come in to me and they say, 'I am glad to meet you, I come from India (or Australia, America, or some other country), and I am a good Congregationalist'; or others come and say, 'I am a good Methodist', or 'I am a Baptist', and immediately I feel there is no union. But others come, and they do not tell me whether they are Baptist, or Methodist or Congregationalist, they just come in and say, 'What a wonderful Lord we have! Thank God this is the same gospel here as in my home country, and my home town!' And immediately I am one with them. We are related, we are in the same family, there is a fundamental union of Spirit. I feel that I have known them all my life, and that if I were to meet them again in the future, I would never be more close to them than at that first moment. That is the unity our Lord talks about; it is not an external matter, nor a matter of denomination or organisation.

Let me go further. If you were to abolish all these denominations, you still would not create unity, because these people who come and say they are good Congregationalists, or good Baptists, and so on, would still be the same sort of people, and by doing away with these distinctions you would not change them. If they came to see you, they would still not be able to talk about this wonderful Lord, they still would not be able to exchange spiritual experiences, because they would be essentially the same people. To think of unity in these external terms is to depart from the glory of our Lord's petition, this unity of faith and belief, this unity of spirit, which is the result of believing the truth and of being made one with the Lord Jesus Christ and therefore one with one another.

If that is true, then, let us move on to my third proposition and consider briefly the things that hinder or break the unity. First of all, you can do that in the matter of the faith; there is nothing that so breaks the unity as a deviation from any part of the word of God. We believe the whole word of God, and to leave out certain parts of it immediately breaks the unity. 'Ah,' they say, 'you must not be particular, the thing is for you who call yourselves Christians to pray together.' But is it not rather important that we should all be praying in the same relationship? How can I pray in unity and in fellowship with a man who may tell me he can go direct to God without the Lord Jesus Christ at all? There are many people who say things like that. They do not see that the only way to enter into the holiest of all is by the blood of Jesus, and not only do they not mention the blood, they do not mention Jesus either. They say, 'You can start listening and talking to God just as you are.' But I say that I have only one way of entering into the holy, eternal Presence, and that is by the blood that was shed for me. Without it I cannot approach God, I dare not approach him. So I cannot respond to these sentimental appeals to start praying together because I must know the basis of my prayer and be certain that I really am accepted of God.

But there is another way – the opposite, in a sense, to that last one – which defeats fellowship and unity; it is this: addition to the word and demanding things that are not demanded in the word. That is why I have no fellowship with the Roman Catholics. Up to a point I am with them, but then they put in their plus – I must believe certain things about the Virgin Mary, etc. But I do not believe these things and I say that to do so is to deny the gospel of the glorious liberty of the children of God. Thank God, there are people even among the Roman Catholics with whom I can have fellowship, but they are those who do not hold to the whole Catholic teaching; they believe in the centralities, and they leave out the additions.

But let me go one step further. We can break the unity in this matter of faith by exalting things to the first position which should be in the second or third place. There are certain great doctrines about which there never has been unity in the Christian church and I take it there never will be, but I would not separate from any brother or sister on matters like that. If I am not certain, I am prepared to be charitable; I stand for certainties, not for things that are doubtful or uncertain. 'In things essential, unity; in things doubtful, liberty; in all things, charity.'

In the same way, the unity can be broken because of the way we live and conduct ourselves. A person's self-assertion always upsets fellowship, so if my spirit is wrong I am making fellowship impossible, and, as I have already said, exalting matters that are secondary. Take, for instance, the church at Corinth. The thing that divided the church was their emphasis on personalities: some of Paul, some of Apollos, some of Cephas. They were worshipping men, arguing about which was the best preacher of the three, getting excited, and forgetting the message because of the men. And if we do that, we are upsetting the unity and fellowship, we are bringing in something that causes a barrier – and that is schism.

And yet another way in which we can break up the unity is in boasting of spiritual gifts. If we single out a spiritual gift and say that it is absolutely essential for everyone, we are breaking the fellowship, because if you read 1 Corinthians 12, you will find that the Holy Spirit dispenses these gifts to different people as he wills. But we must all have the Spirit and manifest him in our lives. So in practice we can break the unity by failing to demonstrate the faith. Any member of the church who falls into grievous sin is also breaking the unity; immediately that happens, there is a break, so failure in conduct and behaviour can do it too.

My last word you can work out for yourselves – it is in many ways the glory of it all. What is the function and purpose of the union? Our Lord answers this question: 'That they all may be one; as thou, Father, art in me, and I in thee, that they also may be one in us: that the world may believe that thou hast sent me' (v. 21). But he adds another answer in the twenty-third verse, and this is one of the most glorious things in the realm of Scripture. Have you ever seen that when you have read this chapter? Why is this union of ours so important? It does not say that if we all become one, then the whole world will believe on Christ – that is patently contradicted in Scripture. But what it does say is this, 'That they may be made perfect in one' – not that the world may believe on me, but – 'that the world may know that thou hast sent me', which is a very different thing. To me, it seems almost childish to be told that if only you were to do away with your denominations then the world would suddenly believe in Christ and everybody would be converted. What a pathetic valuation! You could have one great world church, and there would still be unbelievers, as there are now. The world did not believe when the Son of God was here and speaking with his own lips. No, he does not pray for them, he prays that the world may know that God has sent him. In other words, our unity manifests that we are not merely men, but that God has done something to us in Christ, that we are what we are because the Son of God has come into the world and has borne our sins and given us a rebirth, and has sent his Holy Spirit into us – the unity is to manifest that.

And the second thing our unity is to manifest is that God loves us in exactly the same way as he loved Christ. I ask again if we are able to realise that? Do you know that God in heaven at this moment loves you in exactly the same way as he loved his only begotten Son? We know his love for the Son; remember that he loves you in exactly the same way, and you and I are to live in fellowship in order to demonstrate that. Both all together and individually we are to demonstrate that we are the special subjects of God's love. Whatever happens to us, whatever our circumstances, we are to be demonstrators of the love of God. God loved his Son, and though it led him to be persecuted and tempted, though it led him to be scourged, though it led him to be crucified, God still went on loving him, and the Son showed he was still being loved by the way he lived and died. And you and I are to live and die in that way, and the world will look at us and say, 'What are these people? Look at them in their suffering and in their agony. What enables them to be like this?' And the answer is, 'It is the love which God has towards them. They know his love, they are feeding on it and they are being sustained by it.'

That is why we are to be one; we are to demonstrate these things. The early church did it, that is how it impressed the ancient world. Those people, even when they were thrown to the lions in the arena, were still praising Christ and his love. That is the unity our Lord is interested in. That is the unity that shakes the world. It is not a matter of numbers or great organisations, or one mammoth church. This has nothing to do with numbers; it is a unity of the Spirit; just a handful of men living with Christ led to three thousand converts on the Day of Pentecost, and it is always like that. What we need is not a big church, it is a pure church; it is a holy church, it is a truly Christian church. So for myself, I am not interested in any talk or any appeals which put mechanical, external, or organisational unity above the unity of the Spirit, the unity of faith, and the unity which is based on sanctification. *That* is the unity for which our Lord prays; the unity which you and I are meant to exemplify in our individual lives, and in our corporate lives together as members of the church; that we may be one, as God and Christ are one, in that mystic, spiritual, glorious, perfect unity.

12

With Him in the Glory

Father, I will that they also, whom thou hast given me, be with me where I am; that they may behold my glory, which thou hast given me: for thou lovedst me before the foundation of the world (John 17:24).

We come here, in verse 24, to a consideration of the last great petition of our Lord and Saviour Jesus Christ for his followers and disciples. It is actually the last of the petitions which he offered, and, in many ways, the end of the prayer; in the final two verses he again just reminds his Father of the character of these people for whom he is praying: 'O righteous Father, the world hath not known thee: but I have known thee, and these have known that thou hast sent me. And I have declared unto them thy name, and will declare it; that the love wherewith thou hast loved me may be in them, and I in them' (vv.25 and 26). It is, then, the last of the great petitions, and, at the same time, in a remarkable and extraordinary way, it sums up in itself the entire prayer, so that as we look at it, we shall not only be considering the special new request, we shall also be reminding ourselves of certain things which we have been considering regularly as we have worked our way through this glorious and tremendous chapter.

Now as we come to look at verse 24, we must all surely agree that the main trouble with us (I am speaking of Christian people) is that we will not realise the truth about ourselves. In this Christian life there are many problems and difficulties, but more and more it seems to me that most of our problems, indeed, if not all of them, arise simply from the fact that we fail to realise, and to understand and to appreciate as we ought, what is the real truth about us as Christian people. In the Scriptures we have great words such as these in this verse, these exceeding great and precious promises, and they are all for us. They are meant for us, they were spoken for us; many of them are descriptions of us, and yet how little do we grasp this fact, how little do we seem to realise the truth that is enshrined in them and how slow we are to apply these things to ourselves! I have increasingly come to the conclusion that somehow or other our trouble lies in the fact that we do not read our Scriptures properly; that is, we tend to read them without meditating upon them, without taking a firm grip of them and grasping them for ourselves, and realising that these truths are truths about us. It seems perfectly clear that if only we did that our entire lives would be revolutionised, indeed our whole demeanour would be entirely changed. You cannot read the New Testament without coming to the conclusion that God's people are meant to be full of the spirit of joy and rejoicing. One of our Lord's last words with respect to them was that they might know his joy and peace, that seemed to be his supreme concern, as it is here in this verse. And yet how slow we are to realise these things. We are content to think of ourselves in ways that are far removed from the New Testament description of the Christian, and our experiences are correspondingly far removed from what our Lord has depicted here.

I wonder how many of us can truthfully say that we are rejoicing with 'joy unspeakable and full of glory' (1 Pet 1:8) in the Lord Jesus Christ? We are exhorted to 'rejoice in the Lord alway: and again,' says the great Apostle in Philippians 4:4, 'again I say, Rejoice.' I suppose the final charge which will be brought against us all is the way we have so misinterpreted our blessed Lord by giving the impression that we are living a weary and laborious life, struggling hard against difficulties and obstacles. Indeed, far too often the impression is given that those who are right outside Christianity and the church seem to be very much happier. Now we know that that is merely a matter of appearance, and that in reality such people are not happy at all but profoundly miserable, but by appearance alone you might often gain the impression that they are happier than many of God's people. And the answer to all that is to realise the truth about ourselves, to realise who we are, to realise what we are, to realise everything that the New Testament tells us about ourselves.

In working through this chapter we have been doing that constantly, and now we are going to look at one of the most extraordinary and glorious things of all. Here is our Lord's last petition for his people: 'Father, I will that they also, whom thou hast given me, be with me where I am; that they may behold my glory which thou hast given me: for thou lovedst me before the foundation of the world.' He is about to leave these followers of his; he is going to the cross, to its agony and its shame; he is going to death and to burial, to the Resurrection and to the Ascension, but his concern is about them, and that is what he prays for. So let us look together at this summary of the main teaching of the entire chapter.

First of all, let us look at the One who prays for us. This is the first thing always, the thing we need to grasp before everything else. Here is someone praying to God for us; we people are being prayed for. So who is this who is praying for us? Well, the very terms that he himself uses in this verse tell us who he is. He does not hesitate to address the almighty and eternal God as 'Father', suggesting at once an intimate relationship. In the first verse also he begins by saying, 'Father, the hour is come; glorify thy Son, that thy Son also may glorify Thee.' 'Father': he is indeed none other than the Son of God.

The next word we must look at is the word 'will'. 'Father,' he says, 'I will' – a most astounding word. He does not say, 'I request' or 'I petition' or 'I desire', and it is unfortunate that the Revised Standard Version has translated it as 'desire', for that is not the word, it is much stronger. He says, 'Father, I will,' and we must not reduce that. In other words, here is someone who can come into the presence of the eternal God and say, 'Father, I will, that these may be with me where I am,' at once suggesting, of course, an equality with God; with reverence, he says 'I will' to the almighty Father.

And then, of course, the other phrase that tells us exactly the same thing about him is this phrase 'before the foundation of the world': 'For thou lovedst me before the foundation of the world.' He has said that before, earlier in this prayer: 'And now, O Father,' he says in verse 5, 'glorify thou me with thine own self, with the glory which I had with thee before the world was.' We must not stay with this now, but unless we grasp it, we shall not be able to learn the great lessons of this phrase. He is praying there for us, because, remember, he is not only praying for his immediate followers – 'Neither pray I for these alone, but for them also which shall believe on me through their word' (v. 20). He is praying for Christians in all places and at all times, everywhere; and the One who is praying there for us is none other than the eternal Son of God. That is the whole basis of our standing and our position; we are Christians today because he came from heaven to earth and took upon himself the likeness of sinful flesh and did all that is recorded of him in these Gospels. A Christian, therefore, primarily, by definition, is one who is being prayed for by the eternal Son of God.

Furthermore, at the same time you cannot help noticing at the same time his concern for us. If only we realised that, when besieged and attacked by the devil and sin and temptation! As we face certain difficulties in the Christian life which trouble and perplex us, and, too, the difficulties which we have with ourselves and with other people, our tendency is to feel that we are quite alone and that no one understands. But to all that the answer is that here is the Son of God under the very shadow of the cross, knowing what is before him, and yet his great concern, his primary concern, is for his people. You would have thought he would be spending all his time praying for himself, but if you look at this prayer you will notice that the first five verses only are devoted to himself, the remainder are devoted entirely to this intercession of his on behalf of his followers. There is nothing that is more important for us to grasp than the fact that our Saviour is the eternal Son of God, that he prayed for us on earth and that at this moment he is interceding for us at the right hand of God's glory and power in heaven.

What, then, does he say about us? We have seen the truth about the One who prays, so the second thing we must ask is, what is true of us? Once more we find the answer in this phrase which our Lord has used frequently in this prayer: we are described as 'those whom thou hast given me'. 'Father, I will that they also, whom thou hast given me, be with me where I am.' Christian people are those whom God the Father has given to his Son. You remember how he puts it earlier on where he says in verse 6, 'Thine they were, and thou gavest them me; and they have kept thy word.' I do not know of anything more comforting than this. I, as a Christian, am one of God's chosen people. It is the great doctrine of the Scriptures, you find it everywhere; and our Lord actually repeats it seven times in this last prayer to his Father. These are the people whom God had chosen before the foundation of the world, people belonging to God, and he has given them to his Son, the Lord Jesus Christ. Is there anything more wonderful than this?

Then you note that we are the special object of God's interest and concern. He knew us even before we were born, before he ever made man or created the world, he had these people whom he had chosen, and there he gave them to the Son. As we have seen, there was a great meeting of the Trinity in eternity, and the Father gave these people to the Son and he sent him on this great mission of preparing them for the eternal enjoyment of God.[1] That is what Christianity means, just that; that is why the Son of God ever came into this world. All mankind had sinned and had fallen away from God, and were outside God's life and love. God sent his Son into the world to do certain things for these people whom he had given him, and everything that the Son did in this world he did for these people, he did for us. God sent him for that purpose. As our Lord himself has already pointed out,

---

[1] See Volume 1, *Saved in Eternity* (Kingsway Publications 1988.)

'... thou hast given him power over all flesh, that he should give eternal life to as many as thou hast given him' (v. 2). So he is able to turn to his Father and say, 'I have glorified thee on the earth: I have finished the work which thou gavest me to do' (v. 4), and now he says he is going back to the Father.

Now if you are a Christian, that is what is true of you. All along you have been the special object of God's interest and concern; he has loved you to the extent that he even sent his Son from heaven to earth for you, even to the death of the cross that you might be truly one of his people, that you might have a new nature, a new life, that you might be fitted for standing before him and enjoying him throughout eternity. 'They whom thou hast given me.' Then you notice that negatively we are contrasted with the world. Our Lord has done this throughout the prayer: 'I pray for them: I pray not for the world, but for them which thou hast given me [out of the world]; for they are thine' (v. 9), and now he goes on in verse 25, 'O righteous Father, the world hath not known thee' – so he is not concerned about them at this point – 'but I have known thee, and these have known that thou hast sent me.' 'These' – who are they? They are obviously not of the world, they are separated, taken out of this present evil world, and given to our Lord, as God's chosen and special people.

Now the aspect of this that I would stress at this point is the comfort of it all; the comfort of knowing for certain that we are in this wonderful and blessed relationship to God. Do we meditate upon this truth? Do we think about it, do we rejoice in it as we should rejoice? Let me repeat, we see here the very Son of God just before the end, and this is the thing that is uppermost in his mind; these 'people whom thou hast given me', these people for whom I am going to die, these people I am going to save by giving my life a ransom for them. 'Father,' he says, 'I will' this thing concerning them. But the question is, do we recognise ourselves? Do we know ourselves in these terms? Is it not the case that far too often we think of ourselves as men and women who decide to be righteous, or to be Christian; we have taken it up, and we are going to do this? But before you and I were ever born we were chosen of God and given to the Lord Jesus Christ. He came into the world because the Father had given you and all other Christians to the Son, in order that he might rescue and redeem them; and he has come and has done that and you are one of his people purchased by his precious blood. Oh the tragedy of failing to realise these things! The tragedy of trusting to ourselves and our own activities so much that we lose sight of the most precious truth of all!

We have considered, then, the One who prays, and the people for whom he prays and so now our third question must be: what does he pray for us? You will remember that in going through this chapter, we have seen certain petitions: he prays that we may be kept from the evil that is in this world, and the Evil One at the back of it all; that we may be kept from the devil and his machinations, that we may be kept from his subtle power and jealousy and everything that he would do to separate us from God. Our Lord prays that we may be kept from that; and then, positively, he prays that we may be sanctified, that we may be made more and more fit for God. And that is the way to look at our lives in this world as Christians. This world is a preparation for the next, we are being prepared for glory – that is sanctification. We are being separated from the world and sin, we have been separated to God and brought more and more into fellowship and communion with him: 'Holy Father, sanctify them through thy truth.' And then he prays that we may maintain the spiritual unity into which he has brought us by the rebirth and the gift of the Holy Spirit. This is not a mechanical external unity but an inner, spiritual, vital, organic unity and he prays that it may be preserved. And having prayed all that, he comes to this last and most glorious prayer of all in which he expresses his will.

In other words, in this prayer our Lord has dealt with our past, he prays for our present, and he also deals with our future. The Christian life is a life that is catered for in its entirety, that is the great glory of it:

> The past shall be forgotten,
> A present joy be given,
> A future grace be promised,
> A glorious crown in heaven.

So says the hymn, and here our Lord is now, looking into the future, looking in through the veil, and giving us a glimpse of what awaits us. You see how in every respect he has catered for us. He has interceded on our behalf while we are still alive in this world, but he does not stop at that, he goes on; and as he wills this for his followers, he incidentally teaches us with respect to our own glorious and wondrous future.

What, then, is the future that awaits us as Christians? Let me remind you again of our tragic failure to realise the truth about ourselves. What is it that awaits us when we come to die? I want to put this message to you by way of contrast at this point. As contrast at this point. As I was preparing this very message I happened to read a passage in a daily newspaper, under the heading 'These great words'. And the 'great words' were these:

I love to consider a place which I have never yet seen, but which I shall reach at last, full of repose, and marking the end of these voyages, and security from the tumble of the sea. This place will be a cove set round with high hills on which there shall be no house or sign of men, and it shall be enfolded by quite deserted land; but the westering sun will shine pleasantly upon it under a warm air. It will be a proper place for sleep. The fairway into that haven shall lie behind a pleasant little beach of shingle, which shall run out aslant into the sea from the steep hillside, and shall be a breakwater made by God. The tide shall run up behind it smoothly, and in a silent way, filling the quiet hollow of the hills, brimming it all up like a cup – a cup of refreshment and of quiet, a cup of ending. Then with what pleasure shall I put my small boat round, just round the point of that shingle beach, noting the shallow water by the eddies, and the deeps by the blue colour of them, where the channel runs from the main into the fairway. Up that fairway shall I go, up into the cove, and the gates of it shall shut behind me, headland against headland, so that I shall not see the open sea any more, though I shall still hear its distant noise. But all around me, save for that distant echo of the surf from the high hills, will be silence; and the evening will be gathering already. Under that falling light, all alone in such a place, I shall let go the anchor chain, and let it rattle for the last time. My anchor will go down into the clear salt water with a run, and when it touches I shall play out four lengths or more, so that she may swing easily and not drag, and then I shall tie up my canvas and fasten all for the night, and get me ready for sleep. And that will be the end of my sailing.

'These great words'! Thank God they are not from the Scriptures. They are what the world calls great words and I suppose they are very beautiful in a literary sense, but I thank God that I am not called to preach literature. I will grant, if you like, the beauty of the language, but I cannot think of anything that produces such a striking contrast to the text we are considering together now. Is that the end? Is that what death means for the Christian, to be alone – no man, or anybody – alone, turning a little boat round the corner of the headland from the mighty ocean into this little eddy and there alone you fall asleep and end the voyage? Oh, how I thank God for the Christian gospel! I cannot imagine anything more terrible than that, that is pessimism, that is despair, this desire to be alone. My friend, if you are a Christian, that is not what awaits you, it is this: 'Father, I will that they also, whom thou hast given me, be with me where I am.' You see the contrast – the Christian desire is *not* to be alone, regarding that as supreme bliss, it is to be where Christ is – '... where I am.'

Where are we going? Are we going into some silent place surrounded by wonderful hills and the shimmer of the light upon the waves? No, that is not the gospel! We are going where Christ is: '... to be with Christ; which is far better' (Phil 1:23). To the Christian death does not mean being alone, it means going on to be with him. That is what he said, you remember, to the thief dying by his side upon the cross: 'Today,' he said. You are not going into some little eddy, and there be alone and put down the anchor, and fall asleep – 'Today shalt thou be with me in paradise' (Lk 23:43) '… to be with Christ; which is far better.'

And you notice that our Lord is very concerned here to impress upon us that not only shall we be with him but that we shall *all* be with him: 'Father, I will that they also, whom thou hast given me, shall be with me where I am' – I believe it actually means the total aggregate of Christians, the whole company of the redeemed, all of us together will be with him; we do not look forward to being alone at last, no longer buffeted by other people, and thinking, 'Thank God, at last I'm alone!' – not a bit of it. That is a travesty of the gospel which merely appeals to the natural mind because of the beauty of its language. What the Christian looks forward to is this:

> Ten thousand times ten thousand
> In sparkling raiment white,
> The armies of the ransomed hosts,
> Throng up the steeps of light,
> 'Tis finished, all is finished,
> Their fight with death and sin,
> Fling open wide the golden gates,
> And let the victors in.
> *Henry Alford (1810–71)*

The very essence of the Christian position is that Christians want everybody to share what they have, and they look forward to heaven and to being with all the ten thousand times ten thousand. That is heaven; not to be alone, thank God, but to be among this ransomed throng of the redeemed, safely gathered in, all who have been with us here on earth sharing Christian fellowship, joining with us in song – the saints who have gone before us, the saints who come after us, we all will be there together. What a wonderful vista, what a vision of glory! That is what he wills, '… that they' – all of them – 'may be with me where I am.'

And what shall we be doing there? Well, this is what he says, 'Father, I will that they also, whom thou hast given me, be with me where I am; that they may behold my glory, which thou hast given me.' It is a great word, this word 'behold'; to behold means to gaze upon as a spectator, but it also means to gaze upon some extraordinary sight, something quite exceptional and unusual. We often have that kind of experience, do we not? Maybe we are out walking and suddenly we turn a corner and see some marvellous sight; we behold, we gaze, we stand and look – it is there, in our Lord's phrase, multiplied by infinity. But this word goes even further than that. It is a continuous word – 'that they may continually behold my glory'; we go on beholding! That is not the whole of heaven, of course, but it is perfectly clear from the Scriptures, and especially from the book of Revelation, that this is one of the main things in heaven: to look at the Lord Jesus Christ, to gaze and gaze upon him, to behold him, yes, and very specially, he says, to behold his glory.

Now this is very important. He says, '... that they may behold my glory, which thou hast given me.' We must understand this clearly. Again, as we saw in our last study, it obviously cannot mean his inherent eternal glory as the Son of God, because that was not given to him. He is from eternity the eternal Son of God, co-equal with his Father in glory and in everything else, so it cannot mean the glory which is inherent in the Son of God, as the Son of God. The glory of which he speaks here must be that glory which was given to him after he returned from earth into heaven with his human nature. You see, he came out of heaven and took on him human nature. He went back into heaven God–Man. He did not leave human nature behind when he went back to heaven, he took it with him, so that one who is truly human is at the right hand of God's authority and power in heaven. He went back as God–Man, and a special glory was given to him as the God–Man and the Saviour of his people.

Paul deals with that in Philippians 2, in his great statement about the Incarnation. You remember how he tells us that our Lord had gone back to heaven, and then he says, 'Wherefore God also hath highly exalted him.' Paul has talked about how our Lord 'made himself of no reputation', as Man, he humbled himself, wherefore, because of this, 'God hath also highly exalted him and given him a name that is above every name that at the name of Jesus every knee should bow of things in heaven, and things in earth ...' That is the glory, this peculiar glory that God has given to his Son because of what he has done for us men and women and for our salvation.

And what our Lord wills here is this: he speaks to his Father and he says in effect, 'Father, I am looking forward to this.' As the author of the epistle to the Hebrews puts it, 'Who for the joy that was set before him ...' (Heb 12:2) he saw it, he knew what was coming. So here he turns to his Father and says, 'Father, I will ...' They have seen me here in the flesh, they have seen me as a man of sorrows and acquainted with grief; they have seen me as one who had 'no place to lay his head'; they will see me with the crown of thorns upon my brow and they are going to look upon me with blood oozing out of my hands and my side. They have seen me in the days of my humiliation and have believed on me, Father, and I would that they should see me thus also, see me in my glory and gaze and gaze upon me as I truly am, and as I shall be. That is what is awaiting you and me.

But let me go on and complete this, for I find in 1 John 3:2 that to see this glory of his also means to share it: 'It doth not yet appear what we shall be: but we know that, when he shall appear, we shall be like him; for we shall see him as he is.' In other words, you cannot look at this glory without its being reflected in you; to look at it means to be like it, to be transformed. Paul says the same thing when he says, 'We look for the Saviour, the Lord Jesus Christ: who shall change our vile body that it may be fashioned like unto his glorious body according to the working whereby he is able even to subdue all things unto himself' (Phil 3:20–21). In other words, we look forward not only to seeing and beholding him and looking at his glory, but also to being changed into the likeness and image of his glory.

And still more wonderful of all is the very fact that our Lord wills this for us, which means that it is going to happen to us for certain. You see, it is at this point that we do not understand ourselves; how can we be what we are as Christians? Do you know that you, a humble child, an ignorant Christian, who may feel you are more of a failure than anything else, buffeted by the devil, tossed here and there, do you know that I can tell you this now – you are destined to experience these things, of which we have been thinking. When you come to die, you will be with Christ; you will see his glory, you will behold it, and will become like him, and enjoy the glory for ever and ever. Paul puts it in this way in Romans 8:29–30: 'For whom he did foreknow, he also did predestinate to be conformed to the image of his Son, that he might be the firstborn among many brethren. Moreover whom he did predestinate, them he also called: and whom he called, them he also justified: and whom he justified, them he also glorified.' In the council of God it has already happened, it is as certain as that. You and I, wherever we are at this moment, are going to look into the face of Jesus Christ in all his glory and be made like him and enjoy him through all eternity. That is his will for us, and because he wills it, it is absolutely certain.

The conclusions we draw from this are quite inevitable, are they not? If we all realised these things, would we go on living as we do? Would we be as concerned as we are about this world and its passing pleasures and its glories, its states and pomp and positions? Would we give the time we do give to such worldly things, and so little to this? If we really realised what we are told here, would we be apologetic, sometimes almost afraid for people to know we are Christians? Would we be like that if we believed this; if we knew it was going to happen? But if we are Christians this is going to happen; it is absolutely certain, it is more certain than anything under the sun today that we shall behold him and his glory and become like him.

Whatever, then, you may be doing, put this at the forefront of your mind; think about it in a way that you have never done before; never let a day pass but that you remind yourself of who and what you are. You are one of God's people – 'thine they were, and thou gavest them me' – and I have done for them the work that thou gavest me to do, and I am coming back to thee. 'Father, I will that they also whom thou hast given me, be with me where I am, that they may behold my glory, which thou hast given me' – hold that before yourself day by day, start your day with it, remind yourself of it constantly, 'Set your affection on things above, not on things on the earth' (Col 3:2), for 'our light affliction, which is but for a moment, worketh for us a far more exceeding and eternal weight of glory, while we look' – we gaze steadfastly – 'not at the things which are seen, but at the things which are not seen: for the things which are seen are temporal; but the things which are not seen are eternal. For we know that if our earthly house of this tabernacle were dissolved, we have a building of God, an house not made with hands, eternal in the heavens' (2 Cor 4:17—5:1).

So let us always 'nightly pitch our moving tents, a day's march nearer home'. Oh, do not think of the end of your life in this world as sliding out of the ocean into some little eddy where at last you can be alone. Rather, think of it as going to be with him and with all the ransomed saints, to see and meet people again who were pilgrims with you in this world, and to join with them in singing praises unto him who loved you to the extent of dying for you, and rising again to save you. Think of yourself among the ransomed hosts, the ten thousand times ten thousand, singing for ever and ever the praises of the Lamb who once was slain and who has redeemed us. What a heritage! What a promise! What a hope! What a glory! Blessed be the God and Father of our Lord and Saviour Jesus Christ. Amen.

Sanctified Through
The Truth

by D Martyn Lloyd Jones

How can we live a righteous and holy life in a fallen
and sinful world?

Continuing his exploration into the high-priestly
prayer of Jesus in John chapter 17, Dr Lloyd Jones
shows us that when Christ died to save us, he died to
sanctify us. The very power that raised Christ from
the dead is at work in us, making us holy, from the
moment of our new birth in him.

This has enormous, positive implications for the day-
to-day life of every Christian. For once we discover
that sanctification is not so much a process as a
relationship, we find that we actually want to lead
lives in obedience to God and in fellowship with him.

Sanctified Through The Truth is the third in a series
of four volumes based on John 17.

Kingsway Publications

Safe in the World

by D. Martyn Lloyd-Jones

Christians may understand that their salvation was planned by God from all eternity, yet what difference does this make as we face the trials and temptations of life?

Continuing his exploration into the high-priestly prayer of the Lord Jesus recorded in John chapter 17, Dr Lloyd-Jones shows how we can rely on the Lord Jesus to 'keep us from evil' and also find in him the means to overcome sin, as we base our lives on the unchanging character of our loving Father.

Once again the Doctor demonstrates his singular ability to expound the Scriptures in such a way that our minds are enlightened and our hearts set ablaze, directing us away from a problem-centred approach to life and setting our sights on the One who desires to be glorified in us.

Safe in the World is the second in a series of four volumes based on John 17.

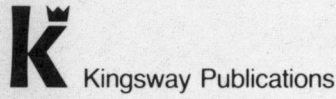

Kingsway Publications